PENGUIN BOOKS

THE PENGUIN METAPHYSICAL LIBRARY
General Editor: Jacob Needleman

THE UNIVERSAL MEANING OF
THE KABBALAH

Leo Schaya was born in Switzerland in 1916
and was brought up in a strictly traditional
Jewish manner. At a very early age he began
to study the great metaphysical doctrines of
both the Orient and the Occident. Because he
was especially interested in learning about Islam
"from the inside," he visited Morocco in 1950,
meeting several of the most influential Sufis.
After his return to Europe he published *The
Universal Meaning of the Kabbalah* and *The
Sufi Doctrine of Unity*. At present he is writing
a vast book of comparative metaphysics. He
describes this work as an illustration of the
biblical words "Have we not all one father?
hath not one God created us?"

LEO SCHAYA

The Universal Meaning of the Kabbalah

Translated from the French by Nancy Pearson

Penguin Books Inc
Baltimore • Maryland

Penguin Books Inc
7110 Ambassador Road
Baltimore, Maryland 21207, U.S.A.

Originally published in French as *L'Homme et l'Absolu
selon la Kabbale* by Editions Buchet/Chastel,
Corrêa, Paris, 1958

English translation first published in Great Britain
by George Allen & Unwin Ltd, London, 1971

First published in the United States
by University Books, Inc., Secaucus, N.J., 1972

Published in Penguin Books 1973
Reprinted 1974

This translation copyright © George Allen & Unwin Ltd, 1971
Foreword copyright © Jacob Needleman, 1973

Printed in the United States of America

THE PENGUIN METAPHYSICAL LIBRARY

The Penguin Metaphysical Library is intended to serve the present need for living ideas—ideas that can move contemporary people to the struggle for self-knowledge. Unfortunately, most of us lack a touchstone by which to recognize these ideas.

The marvels of modern science are the end-result of a movement toward more liberal education and greater freedom of inquiry, which began long ago with the avowed purpose of widening human knowledge. As the pressure of technology increases, however, the authentic patterns of human life are more and more upset, and a descent into total materialism seems to be inevitable. Man has thrust upon himself a standard of knowing and a view of reality which blind him to his possible role within the universal scheme.

Fear and mistrust of the prevailing culture have finally evoked a counterliterature about ancient psychology and esoteric teachings, largely of Oriental origin, which is supposed to reverse the current. Yet it may all be part of the same process. For most of us, the truly wide view of life will remain hidden between the lines. Even the wisdom of great masters, if it does not enter correctly and intimately into our minds, will only burden our already dull and awkward responses with added information.

Man remains, as at all times, an enigma—a "two-natured being," partly divine and partly an animal that reads. Are there special books in this flood of written material that can draw from us, as we read them, the sincerity to listen to the whole truth—books that both help us to awaken to the real meaning of living and bring us a good night's sleep?

In offering a selection from the many available texts, the

editor has necessarily to rely on his own need and hunger for a more impartial sense of himself—a hunger that is far from being permanent or satisfied. His wish is that, at the least, The Penguin Metaphysical Library may help others to hear great ideas in a way that does not support the illusions that have generated the present confusion.

JACOB NEEDLEMAN

Foreword

In the opening pages of this book the author explains that he "has undertaken to rediscover in Judaism the *philosophia perennis* that he learned through the Hindu, Buddhist and Sufi traditions . . . ." He attempts this, however, not through a comparative study of these other religions but solely through an intensive exposition of the Kabbalah. Save for an occasional aside, no other teachings are mentioned in this book.

With his focus on the doctrine of the *Sefiroth*—the aspects of God—the author immediately plunges us into the universal world of ideas. Standing between metaphysical ideas and the symbolic language of the *Zohar* and the Old Testament, he allows each side to penetrate the other. The naturalness and artlessness with which this mutual penetration of idea and symbol takes place are both the demonstration that the author is offering and a lesson to the reader about the lawful results of serious intellectual effort.

This book will be extremely useful to anyone who is, in the words of Maimonides, "perplexed" by the Bible in the sense of having exercised his best thinking about it and who now stands "broken" before its apparent contradictions and its overwhelming emotional authority. Typically, men have sought to resolve the contradictions of the Bible, which Maimonides claimed are there intentionally, by a struggle to commit themselves to one or another meaning, a meaning often selected by ourselves unconsciously. The development of popular religion has therefore tended to mirror in form and act the mind bent on finding answers to biblical puzzles. In Leo Schaya's approach, unity of understanding cannot be found in this way, and we are compelled to suspect that if unity of understanding lies along another scale of mental or

3

emotional effort, then also unity of life must lie there too. The Kabbalah, or esotericism, is the communication to man of what Schaya, following René Guénon and Frithjof Schuon, calls principial ideas—ideas that are to thought and actions what the sun is to its rays.

The cosmic image of the Tree of Life may have been intended to help men realize in their actual lives the possibility of unity in diversity, which in the life of the mind is called the discovery of meaning. The reader must remember, however, that the discovery of universal meaning is also an experiential, bodily, and emotional event requiring three-dimensional sacrifice and need. The ideas in this book make sense only as one glimpses in oneself another state of being, and this state, one may assert, can be glimpsed only as one observes the aspects of oneself that settle for the cheap unities we call happiness.

At the same time that Leo Schaya is so aptly demonstrating the perennial and universal root of Judaism, he is also opening for us a new way of understanding the distinctive and particular emphases it has shown. Such emphases in modern religion have tended to lead into dogma and sectarian rigidity, alienating young and old alike and provoking religious-psychological panic on all sides. One must be grateful, therefore, to be given a picture of Judaism's individuality without being asked to surrender the understanding of reality which one has received from other sources.

In modern times the individuality of Judaism has to a large extent expressed itself in the idea of God's absolute and unknowable transcendence, and in the idea of His severity and justice. Under the former idea, it has sharply defined itself as being against any path of religious gnosis, emphasizing the domain of morality and ethics. Thus cut off from gnosis, Judaism's moral and ethical stance was allowed to intermingle with the temporal morals and politics of society, sands that shift with the winds; and emphasizing the severity of God, Judaism allied itself with the puritanism and guilt-psychology of the epoch that is now passing away.

As Schaya shows, the unknowability of God means something more well defined and practical than has generally been assumed. The extraordinary interplay of cosmic principles which the Kabbalah describes are invisible and real. Within the universe there moves a living structure of energies and forms knowable only by a consciousness that can perceive them within itself. Thus the particular emphasis on God's unknowability is a call to man to struggle for the knowledge of consciousness, self-knowledge. The universe we see is only a surface, a result, bearing for those who can read it in themselves the signature of an inner hierarchy of intentions. Right action, which is perennially the concern of Judaism, emerges within man's struggle for a harmonious contact with these forces in himself. This view, of course, is the direct opposite of social moralism, which wrongly presupposes the existence of the very freedom that is the product of spiritual struggle. That after all this there still remains the unknowable God becomes a mystery to be respected in the light of conscious service rather than in the darkness of blind faith.

As for the severity of God, Schaya constantly uses the Kabbalah to suggest the interaction, within the form of God's mercy, between "rigour" and "grace":

Grace is called the 'right arm' of God and the law his 'left arm'. Thanks to these two opposite but complementary manifestations, God keeps all creation in balance. . . . Grace, by virtue of its unlimitedness, expands the created being indefinitely to the fullness of its measure . . . but where the cosmic measure comes close to its end, rigour, in extreme contraction, causes the totality of created being to return into its first origin . . . . And so one sees . . . why divine rigour . . . could not be identified with God's anger alone. His anger in fact is no more than a cosmic aspect of his rigour . . . [which] denies all that is not God, the only reality . . . . Rigour [is] the negation of the negation of the only reality . . . . [It is] grace in so far as grace appears negative in manifestation . . . .

What would it mean to understand such ideas in more than scholastic fashion? Perhaps they can be assimilated only in that moment of pure being which is said to accompany man's voluntary acceptance of conditions that destroy his illusions about himself. As for those of us who can only make guesses about this moment of freedom, it is clear from this study that the ideas of Judaism and the communications of the Bible are meant to be aids in our search for it.

JACOB NEEDLEMAN

Preface

To understand the intellectual premises of the Kabbalah or of Jewish esotericism – which are those of esotericism or metaphysics in general – one must be imbued with the idea that its doctrines have spiritual contemplation, pure inspiration, or 'intellectual intuition' as their point of departure and not the autocratic activity of reason. When a merely logical thinking seeks to rise above the plane of phenomena by means of abstraction with the object of grasping their transcendent principle, it is led to recognize its own limits – set by the conditions of discriminative knowledge – and its impotence to overcome them; not that it does, in fact, always recognize them, otherwise there would be no philosophical systems, but its very difficulties prove that constructing theories is not enough for the purpose of grasping reality in itself. Now, only doctrines that are traditional and therefore 'inspired' go beyond the vicious circles of mental activity and show the way out towards pure, universal and 'uncreated' Intellect.

As we are taught by the Kabbalah – and also, in the most direct way possible, by Neo-Platonism and the Vedānta – the spirit, while transcending the soul, resides in its depths. The soul and all formal or separate manifestations, whether internal or external, proceed from it, but the spirit itself is formless and without distinction; in it, the subject and the object of knowledge are one: the spirit knows itself completely, it is total knowledge and all that is knowable in itself and in things. Thought, on the other hand, is only an individual and formal plane reflecting the intelligible; it is always in motion between a mental subject, or that which thinks, and a mental object or that which is reflected in thought. But what is reflected in thought is assimilated by it only in its mental form, not in its concrete form – whether corporeal or subtle – and most certainly not in its supraformal, spiritual and universal reality; thus thought is the psychic and rational mirror of all intelligible things, a mirror which never becomes what it reflects. Thought by itself, therefore, does not permit the thinker to assimilate the reality of the mental object: it remains a symbolic knowledge of things, a knowledge which brings the thinker closer to them, but does not really identify him with them. Thought allows the dualism between subject and object to persist to such a point that the man who only knows himself by thought has not truly assimilated himself; he does not really know himself and sees himself only as his own mental form, as the thought or image that he makes of himself. This dualism inherent in thought is the cause of doubt and error; spirit, on the contrary, is the real unity of the cognitive subject and object, and this unity is certitude, the truth of knowledge.

Truth cannot be discovered, therefore, by thought alone, by a faculty which, because of its dualistic nature, cannot pass completely beyond the abyss of its own doubt; as against this, man cannot discover truth without any help from thought, since he is a thinking being, and, if thought had no relation to truth, man would not have any conscious link with it either. One thing is certain: a mental notion of truth exists; thought opposes it to error and identifies it with the concept of reality. This indicates, *ad extra*, a relation between thought and truth, a 'relation' which, *ad intra*, is none other than the spirit. It is the spirit that leads to truth. Thought is the link between man and the spirit, but, at the same time, interposes itself as an obstacle because of its 'organic' dualism, expressed in doubt and error; therefore, thought could not pass beyond error and be integrated in truth without conforming to the spirit and being finally effaced in it.

'Let the wicked forsake his way, and the man of iniquity his thoughts; let him return to YHVH[1] and he will have compassion upon him; and to our God, for he will abundantly pardon. For my

---

[1] The tetragrammaton YHVH represents the sacrosanct name of God in the Jewish tradition. For more than two thousand years the Jews have been forbidden to pronounce this name, and its vocalization is no longer known.

thoughts are not your thoughts, and your ways are not my ways, saith YHVH. For as the heavens are higher than the earth, so are my ways higher than your ways, and my thoughts higher than your thoughts' (Isaiah 55:7–9).

Divine thought, the eternal and supreme archetype of human thought, has two essential aspects: on the one hand, it is meta-cosmic 'wisdom', on the other, it is cosmic 'intelligence'. God, by his wisdom, knows his unmanifested and infinite reality; by his intelligence, he knows his manifestation and the creation issuing from it, which is limited and transitory existence. His wisdom determines the uncreated archetypes; his intelligence manifests them as spiritual and supraformal realities, which, in their turn, clothe themselves in subtle substance and gross matter, in order to give birth to the heavens and the earth.

'For as the rain cometh down and the snow from heaven and returneth not thither except it water the earth, and make it bring forth and bud, and give seed to the sower and bread to the eater, so shall my word be that goeth forth out of my mouth: it shall not return unto me void, except it accomplish that which I please and make the thing whereunto I sent it prosper' (Isaiah 55:10–11).

By his thought, which is the first emanation of his causal being, the first ontological irradiation, God determines all things. By his word, which is his first spiritual manifestation, he creates all things and at the same time reveals their reason for being. The word of God is his act of creation, revelation and redemption. All expressible truths are comprised in this divine revelation. In descending to earth, this one and universal word is multiplied into different 'languages' or revelations, addressed to different sections of humanity. The only truth and only reality thus corresponds, under as many sacred forms, to the various comprehensions and temperaments of the great 'types' of the human collectivity.

The idea of the transcendent unity of religions, of the unity manifested at the beginning of time and in the presence of a humanity still united by a single primordial tradition, has been expounded in the works of René Guénon and Frithjof Schuon and also of Ananda Coomaraswamy. They have shown that the essential principles of the various orthodox revelations are identical, a fact which can be discovered by metaphysical penetration of dogmas and symbols; these expressions vary from one religion to another, but in the light of supraformal and universal truth they cease to appear contradictory and blend essentially into the One. Nevertheless, in order to pass beyond dualistic error, which may take as a pretext the contradictory appearances of the different orthodox revelations, their specific outlines should not be blurred by an imaginative syncretism. On the contrary, the differences from tradition to tradition must be strictly respected, for at the root of the very 'uniqueness' of each will be found the common and supraformal unity of them all: the 'only Father and God'. His purely spiritual, creative and redemptive light is everywhere the same, like that of the sun falling on very different landscapes. That is why, once intelligence passes beyond the formal plane of dogmas and symbols and allows penetration into the kingdom of their formless archetypes, one sees that the clarity of the One is broken only in an extrinsic way into revealing 'rays'. These 'rays', while going in different directions and becoming coloured by different lights, issue from one and the same centre in order to reveal the same mysteries and in order to lead those who assimilate them back to the same origin and end of all things.

To demonstrate this transcendent identity by a metaphysical comparing of religions, is a means of communicating the theoretical knowledge of the truths which lead back to the 'One without a second'; another means is to expound the teachings of one sacred doctrine alone, as has been attempted in this book. The author has undertaken to rediscover in Judaism the *philosophia perennis* that he learned through the Hindu, Buddhist and Sufi traditions, just as it is possible to recognize this same wisdom, under another form, in Christianity also. It is in this spirit of metaphysical universality that the present study has been undertaken, the result of which, so the author believes, can be offered today to the reading public. Although the esoteric tradition of Israel, animated by this same universality, makes it easier to establish a spiritual bridge between the particular and exclusivist[1] form of Judaism and the forms proper to other orthodox religions, there is no occasion to become involved in comparative metaphysics in the framework of the present study, which is devoted solely to the Kabbalah, the 'reception' and transmission of the divine mysteries in the midst of the 'Chosen People'. One can leave to any reader who may be interested the task of establishing for himself the true analogies between the symbolism of the Kabbalistic teachings and that of other traditional doctrines.

Among contemporary interpreters of the Kabbalah, mention should be made of G. G. Scholem, whose work of profound theoretical investigation has rendered it possible to arrive at a global view of Jewish esotericism. However, the Kabbalistic theory still demands much clarification, especially in regard to what transcends the plane of historical and philosophical research. The author in no wise claims to have exhausted the doctrinal wealth of the Kabbalah in the pages that follow, but has concentrated on one of its most essential teachings, dealing with the *Sefiroth*; this concerns the ten principal aspects of God, which, in the form of 'spiritual keys', will help us to look towards his all-reality.

Readers will notice the fact that the study to which this book is particularly dedicated, besides metaphysics and cosmology, is the mystery of the divine Name; here one is concerned not only

---

[1] This 'exclusivism', which denies the other religions and could not have any valid reason other than the protection of Israel's traditional form, was ruptured from time to time, even on the exoteric plane of Judaism, by 'universalist' affirmations on the part of certain of its great representatives, such as Saadya (tenth century), Maimonides (twelfth century), or Yehudah Halevy; on this subject, one need only quote the following remark made by the latter in his dialogue *Al-Khazarî*, written about 1140: 'Christianity and Islam are the precursors and the initiators of the messianic era; they serve to prepare men for the reign of truth and justice . . . '

with the intrinsic aspect of the sacred name, but also with its 'saving' quality. However, it is enough to have limited the author's function to that of theoretician, without entering into questions dealing with method, which are not in his province.

It is said: 'Seek, and ye shall find.'

Contents

1 Torah and Kabbalah

I

All the light that God has given to Israel is hidden in the Torah (law, doctrine or direction); the Torah is the crystallization and mysterious permanence of the Sinaitic revelation. On Sinai, the real presence of *hokhmah*, divine 'wisdom', appeared before the 'Chosen People': 'Israel penetrated the mystery of *hokhmah*', says the *Zohar*,[1] and 'on Sinai the Israelites saw the glory (or real presence) of their (divine) King face to face'.

Now the descent or revelation of the first Tables of the Torah must be distinguished from the second. The *Zohar* teaches that the first Tables emanated from the Tree of Life, but that Israel, by worshipping the golden calf, 'was judged unworthy of benefiting from them'. Therefore, Moses, following the divine command, gave the people other Tables, 'which came from the side of the Tree of Good and Evil'. The law of the second Tables is in fact made up of positive commandments and negative precepts: 'this is permitted, this is forbidden;' life flows from what is permitted, death from what is forbidden. The first Tables, says the Kabbalah, were the light and doctrine of the Messiah, the outpouring of universal deliverance, the source of eternal life on earth. The

[1] The *Sefer Hazohar*, 'Book of Splendour', is composed of several treatises chiefly in the form of Kabbalistic commentaries on the Torah. Written in a rather distorted form of Aramaic, it claims to be the teaching of Rabbi Simeon ben Yohai (second century C.E.) but is generally accepted as the work of the Spanish Kabbalist Moses de Leon (thirteenth century); it is the most widely known and influential work in all the esoteric literature of Judaism. Regarded by many Jewish mystics as a collection of inspired texts this book was often called the 'Holy *Zohar*', and venerated equally with the Torah and its canonical commentary, the Talmud. (The quotations from the *Zohar* are, with a few exceptions, taken from the English translation by H. Sperling and M. Simon, The Soncino Press, London 1949.)

second Tables represented the indirect or 'fragmented' manifestation of this light; *hokhmah*, pure and redemptive wisdom, was no longer immediately accessible, but was hidden behind the 'curtains' of *binah*, the cosmic 'intelligence' of God.

The manifestation of the 'uncreated Torah' had changed, but not its essence, *hokhmah*. The real presence of divine wisdom dwells in the second manifestation as in the first, with the difference that in the second case man is prevented by *binah* 'from advancing his hand, taking from the Tree of Life, eating from it and living eternally'. In order to gain access to *hokhmah*, he must 'cultivate the soil' of his soul by discriminating between good and evil and by practising the divine law; and he must seek with great zeal the truth hidden behind the letters of the Scriptures.

Spiritual penetration of the Written Doctrine (*Torah Shebikh-tab*) is facilitated by the Oral Doctrine (*Torah Shebal-peh*), the second being the explanation of the first. The two doctrines represent the two inseparable – and 'simultaneous' – aspects of the Mosaic revelation. The Written Torah, or static 'letter', serves as the unchanging point of departure for spiritual contemplation of revealed truth; such contemplation could not be effective without the traditional interpretation of the 'letter engraved in stone'; the interpretation, the Oral Doctrine, is 'like a hammer which shatters the stone', thus freeing from it the spiritual 'sparks' of *hokhmah* which dwells within it.

The simultaneous revelation of the Written and of the Oral Torah is based on the Scriptural verse (Exodus 20:18): 'And all the people perceived the thunderings and the lightnings and the voice of the horn and the mountain smoking.' The *Zohar* comments on this verse by saying that the divine words were imprinted on the darkness of the cloud that enveloped the real presence of God, so that Israel at the same time heard them, as Oral Doctrine, and saw them, as Written Doctrine; and the *Zohar* points out that every word was divided into seventy sounds – revealing the seventy fundamental interpretations of the Scriptures – and that these sounds appeared to the eyes of Israel as so many sparkling lights; and, finally, that the precepts of the Decalogue were the synthesis of all the commandments and that at the moment of their revelation Israel penetrated into all the mysteries enclosed in the Scriptures.

2

The Oral Torah is the transmission, from generation to generation, of the mysteries and 'interpretations' contained in the Written Torah as 'sounds' – inspired words – or 'sparkling lights' – spiritual visions. It follows that the saying in *Pirke Aboth* (1, 1): 'Moses received the Torah on Sinai and transmitted it to Joshua, Joshua to the elders, the elders to the prophets and the prophets to the men of the Great Synagogue' refers both to the Written and to the Oral Torah. 'When the Holy One, blessed be he, revealed himself on Sinai in order to give the Torah to Israel, he delivered it to Moses in this order: the Scriptures (the written Torah); the Mishnah, the Talmud, the Haggadah (which, taken together, designate the Oral Torah)' (Exodus *Rabba* 47, 1).[1] Every orthodox oral teaching, even presented as the personal expression of a teacher, goes back to the 'sounds 'and 'lights' of Sinai. 'Even what an outstanding disciple was destined to teach in the presence of his master had already been said to Moses on Sinai' (P. *Peah* 17a).

Now the Haggadah, or the Haggadic Midrashim, form the link between Talmudic or public instruction and the secret teaching

[1] The Written Torah, in the strictest sense, consists of the Pentateuch (*Hamishah Humshei Torah*, the 'five-fifths of the Doctrine', or five books of Moses) and, in the widest sense, also the Prophets (*Nebiim*) and the Writings (*Ketubim*). The Oral Torah includes, on the one hand, the Talmud, the public 'Study' or exoteric commentary on the Scriptures (which consists, in the strictest sense, of the Mishnah or 'Repetition' of the oral teaching, and the Gemarah, 'Complement' or commentary on the Mishnah; and, in the widest sense, also of the Midrashim, rabbinical 'Explanations', and the Haggadah, traditional 'Narration' – historical and symbolic – which includes the non-legal parts of the Gemarah and Midrashim); on the other hand, the Oral Torah comprises the Kabbalah, esoteric commentary on the Scriptures and initiation into the 'Mysteries of the Torah'.

17

of the Kabbalah, the 'reception'[1] of pure wisdom, intended for the spiritual elect of Israel. The Haggadah leads from the 'service of God' to the 'knowledge of the Holy One, blessed be he'. 'Do you desire to know the One who spoke and brought the world into being? Study the Haggadah, for by that you will arrive at the knowledge of the Holy One, blessed be he, and hold fast to his paths' (*Sifre Deuteron.* xlix, 85a).

The Oral Doctrine interprets the Scriptures by four fundamental methods of exegesis that lead to the Kabbalah, to the sphere of *sod*, 'mystery', or, as the Talmud calls it, *Pardes*, the 'Paradise' of divine knowledge. The four consonants of the word *Pardes (PRDS)* themselves designate these four methods, namely: *P=peshat*, the 'simple' interpretation of the Scriptures, approaching it by all the ways available to elementary reasoning; *R= remez*, 'allusion' to the many meanings hidden in every phrase, every letter, sign and point of the Torah; *D=derash*, the 'homiletic exposition' of doctrinal truths, including all possible interpretations of the Torah; *S=sod*, 'mystery', initiation into *hokhmah*, the divine wisdom concealed in the Scriptures and called, insofar as it is a teaching, *Hokhmath Hakabbalah*, the esoteric 'wisdom of the tradition'.[2]

This fourth method, which teaches the 'mysteries of the Torah' (*Sithre Torah*), consists essentially of the spiritual exegesis and application of the first chapter of Genesis, (*Maaseh Bereshith*, the 'Work of the Beginning') and of the first chapter of Ezekiel's prophecies, containing the vision of the divine throne as a celestial 'chariot' (*Maaseh Merkabah*, the 'Work of the Chariot'). But besides these fundamental teachings concerning the emanation from the universal principle and reintegration into it, all of the

---

[1] The word *kabbalah*, derived from *kabbel*, 'to receive', 'to accept', has come to mean secret 'tradition'.

[2] The Kabbalistic method makes use for exegesis among other things, of the science of 'letters' and 'numbers'. The three most highly developed procedures in this science are: *Gematria*, the science of the numerical value of letters; *Notarikon*, the science of the first, the median and the last letters of words; and *Temurah*, the science of the permutation and combination of letters.

Scriptures can serve as a point of departure for the exegetical method of *sod*. The ten *Sefiroth*, 'numerations' or determinations of the divine aspects, play the part in this method of supports for contemplation, whereas the divine names represent the operative means of uniting the Kabbalist – who invokes them according to initiatic rules – with the 'light of Sinai', the real presence of God.

3

As we have just seen, the Kabbalah is the doctrinal essence of the Torah, the repository in the heart of Judaism of the 'mysteries hidden since the beginning of time'. God has revealed these mysteries in many traditional or religious forms; but this diversity is only the expression of the infinite 'richness' of the one truth and in no way affects its transcendent and immutable unity. The Kabbalah is therefore nothing but the Jewish branch of that universal 'tree' of deifying wisdom which is discovered at the base of all orthodox ways leading to pure and integral knowledge. This knowledge of divine truth was given to the patriarchs of Israel and to their chosen disciples and was finally crystallized in the Sinaitic revelation. Moses transmitted it to Joshua, Joshua to the elders, the elders to the prophets, the prophets to the men of the Great Synagogue and they in turn communicated it to the members of the 'chain of (esoteric) tradition' (*shalsheleth hakabbalah*). This 'chain' seems to have remained intact up to our day; it is destined, in fact, to link the wisdom of Adam with that of the Messiah. After the return of the people from Babylon, when prophecy in Israel had come to an end, it was Ezra who, in a definitive way, bequeathed the Torah with its laws and mysteries to the Jewish world. His spiritual legacy was guarded by the 'men of the Great Synagogue', the *Sofrim*— 'scribes'—and their disciples, the members of the 'traditional chain'; the latter transmitted it to the *Tannaim* (first to third century C.E.), who were doctrinal authorities such as the great Kabbalistic masters, Akiba and Simeon ben Yohai. After the death of the last of the *Tannaim,* who was Judah the Holy (the editor of the written Mishnah), the oral doctrine was taught by the *Amoraim* (third to fifth century), those doctors of the *Torah* 'who were no longer authorities in themselves' but repeated and commented on the traditions of the *Tannaim;* their supplementary teachings on the Torah were collected in the Gemarah, the 'complement', or commentary on the Mishnah. The Rabbis or spiritual 'masters' carried on the exoteric and esoteric teaching of the *Amoraim* by 'expositions' (Midrashim) and initiation into the mysteries. At the time of dispersion of the Jewish people, the secret "chain of tradition" went across most of Europe. The teaching of the mysteries of the Torah and the practice of Kabbalistic methods were known through the entire Middle Ages and right down to modern times. The most important collections of the esoteric doctrine of Judaism are the *Sefer Yetsirah,* the 'Book of Formation', the teaching in which is believed to derive from Abraham, and the *Sefer Hazohar,* the 'Book of Splendour', on which the present exposition of the mysteries of Israel is chiefly based. These collections and other authoritative mystical treatises which have been preserved down to our day make it possible to discover the Kabbalah, the true 'reception' of divine wisdom, behind the letters of sacred Scripture.

II Contemplation of the Divine Aspects

A. THE UNITY OF THE *Sefiroth*

I

The *Sefiroth*, the metaphysical 'numbers' or 'numerations' of the divine aspects, are the principal keys to the mysteries of the Torah. They form a tenfold hierarchy and their names, enumerated from the highest downward, are: *kether*, 'crown' (or *kether elyon*, supreme crown); *hokhmah*, 'wisdom'; *binah*, 'intelligence'; *hesed*, 'grace' (or *gedullah*, 'greatness'); *din*, 'judgement' (or *geburah*, 'power', or again *pahad*, 'fear'); *tifereth*, 'beauty' (or *rahamim*, 'mercy'); *netsah*, 'victory' or 'constancy'; *hod*, 'glory' or 'majesty'; *yesod*, 'foundation' (or *tsedek*, 'justice'); *malkhuth*, 'kingdom' or 'royalty' (or *shekhinah*, divine 'immanence'). The *Sefiroth* in their totality constitute the doctrinal basis of Jewish esotericism; they are to the Kabbalah, or mystical 'tradition' of Judaism, what the Ten Commandments are to the Torah, as the exoteric law. The ten *Sefiroth* represent the spiritual archetypes not only of the Decalogue, but also those of all the revelations of the Torah. They are the principial determinations or eternal causes of all things. This decad is divided into nine emanations or intellections by which the supreme *Sefirah*, the 'cause of causes', makes itself known to itself and to its universal manifestation.

It must be understood, however, that the fact that God makes himself known under multiple aspects, does not mean that he is in reality any particular number or multitude; 'he is One and there is no other'.[1] In his all-reality, God includes an indivisible infinity of

[1] This is one of the characteristic formulas of the absolute monotheism of the Jewish tradition. This direct affirmation of the exclusive reality of God is found, for example, in Isaiah (Ch. 45 and 46), where it is repeated many times that 'there is none other' (*en od*) than he. In the chapter entitled 'The return to

eternal possibilities, which is inconceivable for created beings
—except through a revelation at once distinct and synthetic.
Now the *Sefiroth* are, precisely, ten revealed syntheses of the
innumerable and boundless aspects of the only reality; but the
decad is symbolic and does not imply that God has any specific number of attributes. He is beyond all measurement, infinite both in his hidden essence and in his ontological and
revealed qualities. The *Zohar* itself (*Bo* 42b) makes it clear
that the numerical nature of the *Sefiroth* is only relative, by
emphasizing that everything is in God's power 'whether he wills
to lesson the number of (Sefirothic) vessels and (correspondingly)
increase the light which springs from them, or whether he wills
the contrary'. In a word, the Sefirothic decad is nothing other than
the divine unity insofar as it opens itself, in one intelligible mode
or another, before the created multitude.

The *Sefiroth*, therefore, appear to be multiple only in the eyes of
the created multitude; in reality, all the 'numbers', or metaphysi
cal aspects, are integrated without distinction into the One who is
'without number' because he 'has no second'. This truth and others
which summarize the Sefirothic doctrine are expressed in the
following Kabbalistic 'hymn of praise', called the 'prayer of Elijah'
(quoted from the *Tikkune Zohar*): 'Master of the worlds! Thou
art One, but not according to number (for thou art the only
reality). Thou art the sublimest of the sublime, the most hidden of
all hidden things. No thought can conceive thee (in thy pure and
supra-intelligible essence). Thou has brought forth (determined)
ten (supra-formal and principial) forms (representing the eternal
archetypes of all things) which we call *Sefiroth* ("numbers" or
pure determinations), in order to govern through them (which
are the first and intelligible causes) the unknown and invisible
worlds and the visible worlds. Thou didst wrap thyself in them
(as the "cause of causes") and since thou dwellest in them (being

---

the One' of this study, we shall return in detail to this essential doctrine of
Judaism, which, let it be said right away, should by no means be mistaken for
pantheism, in the philosophical and current sense of the term.

their very unity, essential and indivisible), their harmony remains unchanging. To imagine them as divided would be as though to divide thine unity. These ten *Sefiroth* are unfolded by degrees (are manifested hierarchically) . . . Thou art he who governs them, while thou art governed by no one, whether from above or below. Thou madest the clothing (spiritual manifestations) for the *Sefiroth* which serves human souls as means of passage (between their limited world and thine infinite world) . . . Thou didst hide the *Sefiroth* in bodies . . . In their totality they correspond (as archetypes) to the members of the human form (which is the microcosmic "image" of the causal Being and of its aspects) . . . Thou thyself hast neither image nor form in all that in thee (in thine all-reality) is within (non-manifested) or without (manifested) . . . Nobody can know thee in truth (in thine eternally hidden selfness). We know only that there is no unity outside of thee, neither above nor below . . . Every *Sefirah* has a definite name, after which the angels are also named, but thou thyself (unknowable essence) hast no definite name, for thou art the One (the only reality) who fills all names (ineffably, without distinction) and gives them all their real value; if thou wert to withdraw thyself, they would remain as bodies without a soul. Thou art wise, but thy wisdom is boundless. Thou art intelligent, but thine intelligence is without limit. Neither art thou in any one place (since thou art the one and only reality). But all this (the totality of thy being-emanations and cosmic manifestations) subsists in order to make known to man thy strength and thine omnipotence, to show him how the universe is governed by rigour and mercy (the two fundamental regulating principles of created existence). Therefore, (referring to the world of the *Sefiroth*) if a "right side" (symbolizing the aspect of grace) is spoken of, or a "left side" (expressing rigour), and a "centre" (synthesizing the two opposite aspects in the "middle pillar", or principle of universal harmony), this is only a means to describe thy government in the universe in relation to human actions and not to indicate that thou (in thine essential and non-causal state) hast some attribute such as justice, or another, such as grace; such terms (designating different

Sefiroth or first causes and valid only from the subjective point of view of their cosmic effects) correspond to no reality (which could be attributed to thy pure essence, in which there is neither cause nor effect nor any relationship between any two aspects whatsoever, but solely thine absolute unity, thy non-duality).'

2

The objective reality of the *Sefiroth* is their indivisible infinity, their unlimited unity, which implies that every divine aspect is identified with the totality of God and by that very fact with all has aspects; this is not by qualitative confusion but by essential fusion. In the causal unity of the *Sefiroth*, the supreme archetypes, all is all, ontologically speaking; which is to say that there is no separation between one reality of divine being and another; nevertheless, no confusion exists between their respective qualities. All is all, but every *Sefirah* is what it is, in its eternal attribute as in its transitory and multiple reflections. In the world of archetypes, everything is conceived in a divinely perfect order of degrees and states, of great and small worlds, of beings and things, without its being possible yet to discern their inequality as it becomes apparent in the midst of the cosmos.[1] Although every attribute of divine being may have its particular 'place', its particular 'number' in the causal unity of the *Sefiroth*, and although each of them radiates the All in accordance with its own eternal mode, yet essentially all his aspects are nothing other than his one and indivisible light. The hierarchy of the *Sefiroth*, including the hierarchy of universal possibilities, is simultaneously established by purely

[1] Meister Eckhart says: 'The archetypes of all things are equal, although they are the archetypes of unequal things. The highest angel, the soul and the gnat have only one archetype in God (his Being, in which all archetypes are identical) . . . God gives to all things equally and to the extent that things emanate from God, they are equal; yes, angels, men and all creatures are equal as they first issue from God. And he who would take things at their source would see them as all equal. But if they are already so equal in time, how much the more so in God, in eternity. If one takes a gnat as it is in God, it is nobler that the highest angel is in itself (as a creature). In God all things are equal and are God himself.'

ideal succession. The One sees himself in everything and everything in himself in one eternal look. His seeing is his own determination of himself, implying the determination of all his aspects – but in a purely unitive manner. Therefore, in the one and uncreated Being there is at the same time determination and unity of realities; whereas, in dual and created existence the same realities are reflected as distinct and interrelated. It is only in the midst of creation that there exists effective separation and succession of possibilities, that is, a definite hierarchy in which every reality includes, in a determinant or active way, those which proceed from it and, receptively or passively, those from which it issued. Nevertheless, since the 'visible is but the reflection of the invisible', the 'lower order' necessarily corresponds to the 'higher order' in which the filiation of possibilities, as previously pointed out, is established in a purely ideal and principial way in divine 'thought' alone, which transcends all rational and dualistic concepts. In other words, the differentiation and relationship characterizing the causal sequence of the cosmic hierarchy are potential in the world of the *Sefiroth*, as pure determination and ontological unity of all things. The existential separativity of things is only actualized in a limited and transistory way and, thanks to the universal concatenation, returns to principial unity, the 'supreme point' from which it came. 'From this (causal) point (down to the very lowest state of existence), there is extension after extension, each one forming a vestment (manifestation, effect, or "envelope") to the other, being in the relation of membrane and brain (symbolizing the cause, centre, or archetype) to one another. Even while being a vestment (in relation to the preceding expansion which is its immediate cause), each stage (emanation or manifestation) becomes a brain (principle) to the next stage (which is its effect; everything is therefore "brain" or principle for what is lower, and "envelope" or manifestation for what is higher than itself)' (*Zohar, Bereshith* 19b).

Thus the *Sefiroth* themselves appear to be wrapped within one another, in their hierarchic order, and so closely interrelated that nothing but a single principial whole can be perceived. In reality their unity is indivisible: it is the totality of the divine powers, which are expressed in their specific aspects only when they are manifested in the midst of cosmic separativity. All distinct manifestations, all the variety of things, are only the effects and symbolic 'wrappings' of the *Sefiroth*; they are ordered and linked together by the *Sefiroth* and re-absorbed into them, into their unity which is the one, universal cause, the only God.

3

The revelatory, creative and redemptive light of the divine Being is, so to speak, 'refracted' through the causal 'prism' of his aspects, the *Sefiroth*, into the indefinite multitude and variety of universal manifestation. The immense hierarchy of onto-cosmological degrees, with all they contain, is established by this 'refraction' of the divine light; these degrees are recapitulated in the four 'worlds' (*olamim*), namely: *olam ha'atsiluth*, the transcendent 'world of emanation', which is that of the *Sefiroth*; *olam haberiyah*, the ideal or spiritual 'world of creation', filled with the divine immanence (*shekhinah*) alone; *olam ha'yetsirah*, the subtle 'world of formation' inhabited by angels, genii and souls; and *olam ha'asiyah*: the sensory and corporeal 'world of the made fact'.

The one and only transcendent emanation of the *Sefiroth* descends, as purely spiritual and supra-formal immanence, into the two lower worlds – the subtle and the corporeal – where it is 'received' and expressed in different ways, by the multiple nature of cosmic existence. The Sefirothic unity appears there as a decade of archetypes, causing myriads of existential effects, each of which is linked, through the universal hierarchy, to its own cause or *Sefirah* which unites it with the indivisible entity of the divine aspects: the One. He who is the unity or infinity of the *Sefiroth* is reflected on every cosmic level in all possible ways, in ways which intersect one another, are opposed to one another, are interconnected, harmonized and united once more in him, who is common origin. One creation expresses him under the aspect of one *Sefirah*, another under some other aspect; but in reality all things manifest all the *Sefiroth* simultaneously, each thing manifesting them in the light of its own archetype. What is more, an emanation or divine manifestation experienced by one created being as mercy may be experienced by another as rigour, depending on the 'relationship' existing between one or another being and the divine cause. God is grace in one respect, severity in another, and the same is true of all his causal qualities; they are manifested on all levels and in all states of existence in an indefinite variety of ways, although he himself is eternally and infinitely the One, the Unchangeable.

' . . . when he shows forth his power to rule over the whole of his creation, appearing, therefore, to each of his creatures according to the capacity of each to comprehend him . . . in order that he might be known by his attributes and perceived in each attribute separately . . . that it may be made manifest that the (differentiated) world is sustained by mercy and by justice (the two qualities of "lordship" which include all the others), according to the works (and good or bad attitudes) of men. . . . But woe unto the man who should presume to compare (the absolute essence of) the Lord with any (specific) attribute (existing only from the point of view of cosmic and dualistic "illusion"), even one which is his own, much less any human created form, "whose foundation is in the dust" (Job 4:19) . . . The only conception of the Holy One, blessed be he, which man dare frame is of his sovereignty over some particular attribute or over creation as a whole. And if we perceive him not under those manifestations, there is left neither attribute, nor similitude, nor form in him (in his pure and unlimited ipseity); even as the sea, whose waters have neither form nor tangibility in themselves, but only when they are spread over a certain vessel which is the earth' (*Zohar*, *Bo* 42b).

God, in his pure reality, is absolutely non-dual and the multitude of his aspects or emanations, whatever their respective quality may be, exist only in the view of the emanated, which is in a state of relative and illusory 'separation'. This applies to the human and individual being, who experiences his own uncreated

and infinite essence only through the intermediary of the lower
Sefirah, divine immanence or 'glory', which cares for created beings
'as a mother cares for her children'. Thus the *Zohar* (loc. cit.) says:
'Had the brightness of the glory of the Holy One, blessed be his
name, not been shed over the whole of his creation, how could he
have been perceived even by the wise ? He would have remained
(totally) unapprehendable, and the words "The whole earth is full
of his glory" (Isaiah 6:3) could never be spoken with truth.' But
the closer man comes to his pure and divine essence, the more he
experiences the intrinsic unity in all the emanations of the *Sefiroth*;
for this unity is none other than the essence of man, the supreme
'self': 'All (Sefirothic) grades and all (existential) members (of the
only reality) were gathered there and became in it one without any
separation' (*Zohar, Bereshith*, 18a).

4

The infinite and indivisible unity of the *Sefiroth* is the very fact
which made it impossible for the Kabbalists to be content with
only one representation of the Sefirothic hierarchy. The essential
and unlimited identity of the *Sefiroth* gives rise, on the level of
differentiation, to innumerable relationships between their static
aspects, and consequently to the possibility of contemplating
them from a multitude of 'points of view' corresponding to these
very relationships.

Thus, to give a few fundamental examples, the Sefirothic unity
can be contemplated *ad intra* by regarding all its aspects as enclosed in *kether*, the supreme *Sefirah*, which is identical with *en sof*,
pure 'infinity'. In this case, the Sefirothic hierarchy is imagined in
the form of concentric circles, the outermost of which is surrounded by *kether*, and the innermost of which contains *malkhuth*, the
last of the *Sefiroth* (see p. 29, Fig. I). From this point of view, the
'cause of causes', or the 'supreme will', concentrates his 'thought'
(epithet of *hokhmah*) on his universal 'kingdom', *malkhuth*, in
order to create the cosmos; or in other words, *kether*, the infinite,
is 'contracted' by *tsimtsum*, the 'drawing together' of the *Sefiroth*,

REPRESENTATIONS OF THE UNITY OF THE TEN *SEFIROTH*

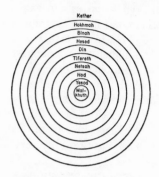

Fig. I. Divine Concentration (or *Sefirothic* Emanation, seen *ad intra*)

Fig. II. Divine Radiation (or *Sefirothic* Emanation, seen *ad extra*)

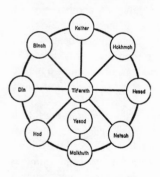

Fig. III. The 'Union' of the *Sefiroth* in the 'Heart' of God (*Tifereth*, inasmuch as it harmonizes and synthesizes all the other *Sefiroth*)

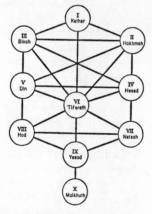

Fig. IV. The 'Tree of the *Sefiroth*' (Representing the hierarchy from the standpoint of prototypical position and relationship)

until the uncreated and creative substance, *malkhuth*, is actualized and gives birth within itself to all the worlds of the cosmos. On the other hand, the Sefirothic 'world of emanation' can be contemplated *ad extra*, taking the same symbolism of concentric circles as support, but this time placing *kether* in the centre and *malkhuth* on the periphery (see p. 29, Fig. II). In this case, *kether*, the infinite, becomes the 'point', the supreme or innermost 'centre', enveloped hierarchically by all its ontological emanations and cosmic manifestations; *malkhuth*, which surrounds the outermost circle, as the *shekhinah* or 'divine omnipresence', then, contains the whole of creation. So, if one looks 'inwards' God creates the world by 'contraction' or 'concentration' of his ontological possibilities, and if one looks 'outwards', by their 'expansion' or 'radiation'.

Now, these two figures emphasize particularly the centripetal and centrifugal aspects of the Sefirothic hierarchy, without taking into account the 'relationships' by which its members are connected between themselves. This is shown in another circular symbol reproduced in Figure III. Here, the centre of the *Sefiroth* is represented by the 'medial' *Sefirah*, *tifereth*, divine 'beauty', also called the 'heart' of God, because it connects, harmonizes and unites his rigour with his grace, as well as all his other opposite aspects, whether those of the 'right' and of the 'left' or those 'above' and those 'below'.

But the most classical arrangement of the *Sefiroth* is the fourth one (see p. 29, Fig. IV) although here again many variants exist as regards the 'channels' connecting each *Sefirah* to all the others. According to this arrangement, the tenfold unity of the *Sefiroth* is shown as a hierarchy of three triads projected into their common recipient, namely, the tenth and last *Sefirah*, *malkhuth*, which is the immediate cause of the cosmos. The highest triad, *kether-hokhmah–binah* (crown–wisdom–intelligence), is that of the essential and ontological principles; the second triad, *hesed–din–tifereth* (grace–judgement–beauty), is that of the cosmological principles; the third, *netsah–hod–yesod* (victory–glory–foundation), is that of the cosmic powers and the creative act; finally, the

Sefirah malkhuth (kingdom), as we have already said, is the un-created and creative substance, or, viewed under another aspect, divine immanence. Elsewhere, these four Sefirothic degrees are respectively the archetypes of the 'four worlds' of transcendent 'emanation', prototypical 'creation', subtle 'formation', and sensory 'fact'. In this way, the tenfold unity of the *Sefiroth* is revealed as the 'hierarchy' of the universal government of God.

The same symbolism shows the Sefirothic unity in the form of three other triads, which also end in the tenth *Sefirah*, *malkhuth*, and constitute the divine 'modes of government'. God reigns through his 'right arm' or 'right side', which 'embraces life and mercy'; through his 'left arm' or 'left side', which contains 'death and rigour', and through the 'middle pillar', which balances, har-monizes and resolves all oppositions in its unity. The 'right' or merciful 'side' comprises the *Sefiroth hokhmah*, undifferentiated 'wisdom', *hesed*, unitive 'grace', and *netsah*, 'victory' or the affirmative cosmic power. The 'left' or severe 'side' comprises *binah*, discriminative 'intelligence', *din*, 'judgement', which separates one reality from another, and *hod*, 'glory' or the negative cosmic power. Finally, the 'middle pillar' is made up of *kether*, 'crown', or unity of *hokhmah* and of *binah*; *tifereth*, 'beauty', or the unity of *hesed*, 'grace', and of *din*, 'judgement'; *yesod*, the cosmic 'founda-tion', or the creative act, which unites the affirmative and nega-tive powers of the cosmos, that is *netsah*, 'victory', and *hod*, 'glory'; and finally *malkhuth*, 'kingdom', the lower unity, recipient of all the divine emanations.

There exists an almost organic relationship between the divine 'hierarchy of government', which consists in the numerical 'filia-tion' of the *Sefiroth* and the 'modes of government', grouped according to the respective 'kinship' of the archetypes. The emana-tion of each antinomic *Sefirah*, in order to manifest its own quality through a lower and kindred *Sefirah*, has to pass numerically through the one which is both opposed to it and at the same time its complement. Thus, when *hokhmah*, undifferentiated 'wisdom', wishes to manifest as *hesed* or unitive 'grace', its radiation must first unite with its contrary aspect, *binah*, distinctive 'intelligence', and when the latter wishes to manifest as *din*, or 'judgement', which separates one thing from another, its emanation must first pass through *hesed*, unitive 'grace', and so forth; this is also true for the affirmative and negative cosmic powers, *netsah*, 'victory', and *hod*, 'glory', which, in order to be able to manifest in creation, must first be united in *yesod*, the cosmic 'foundation'. The same interpenetration of opposites takes place in the 'middle pillar', where *kether*, the supreme 'head', in order to reveal itself through *yesod*, its creative and redemptive act, must 'consult' its 'heart', *tifereth*; and the latter, which is divine 'beauty', blissfully reposing in 'being', is obliged, in order to be able to radiate into the world, to emerge from itself and express itself through the affirmative and negative forces of the cosmos concentrated in *yesod*, the 'act'. Finally, the latter could produce nothing whatsoever without passing through its opposite and at the same time complementary aspect, *malkhuth*, divine 'receptivity'; and *malkhuth*, in spite of its infiniteness, could give rise to nothing did it not find within itself its antinomic possibility, the 'finite', which serves as its recipient.

Each *Sefirah*, therefore, contains either the seed or the influx of its opposite aspect and can allow itself to be penetrated and integrated by it or the reverse, without one of the other losing thereby its own and immutable distinctness. So long as one regards them from the discriminative and 'multiple' point of view, which is specifically that of the individual being, the *Sefiroth* have to be considered from the angle of their eternal 'co-emanation' and 'co-operation'; if one of them is contemplated singly, all the others have to be regarded as implicit in it, and in the light of its own particular quality. This Sefirothic law, which prevents 'excess' in the manifestations of one particular archetype and guarantees balance in all the realms of creation, expresses more than mere 'harmony' or ontological 'equity', for the latter exists only in respect to cosmic duality; this law rests, above all, on the indivisible 'infinity of the *Sefiroth*', in which all opposites are eternally resolved in the One.

It must be added that the essential and incorruptible unity of the Sefiroth is revealed not only by their reciprocal 'relationships', which are concentrated in the 'middle pillar', but also by their common light which 'circulates' in the 'channels' of these relationships and is called *da'ath*, 'knowledge'. This refers to the omniscience or universal consciousness of God which, properly speaking, is not a *Sefirah*, but the cognitive presence of the One in each of them. In fact, *da'ath* is identified with every aspect of divine consciousness, from *kether's* 'first becoming conscious' which is *hokhmah*, his pure wisdom, down to the last distinct and created reflection of the *Sefiroth*. And yet, considered under the aspect of 'omniscience' alone, *da'ath* becomes in the eyes of the Kabbalists a combined effect of *hokhmah* and *binah*; for it is then divine knowledge, which no longer rests exclusively in contemplation of the One, as does *hokhmah* by itself. *Da'ath* in this case is the knowledge which springs from the union of *hokhmah*, purely ontological wisdom, and *binah*, ontocosmological intelligence, and becomes the common intellection of the seven lower *Sefiroth*, by which universal creation is conceived, constructed and ruled.

But, let it be stressed, just as the 'middle pillar' as well as the 'right side' and the 'left side' of the 'world of emanation' are not superadded to the supreme and immutable decade, so *da'ath* is in no way an eleventh Sefirothic element. This is why the *Sefer Yetsirah* (I, 4–9) never tires of repeating: 'Ten *Sefiroth*, without anything (other whatsoever; for, from the point of view of the Kabbalah, they synthesize all the aspects of God, even his pure essence, which is no longer an "aspect" properly so-called, but the reality of all realities); ten and not nine (for although *kether*, the supreme *Sefirah*, pure essence, is not an emanation like the nine other *Sefiroth*, but the non-emanated principle of all emanation, it is contained in the tenfold unity of the *Sefiroth*); ten and not eleven (since there is no divine principle outside the Sefirothic unity) . . . Ten *Sefiroth*, without anything (other whatsoever); their measures (qualities or attributes) of ten have no limits . . . Ten *Sefiroth*, without anything (other whatsoever); their appearance is like lightning and their aim is without end . . . Ten *Sefiroth*, without anything (other whatsoever); thou shalt con-

33

nect their end (the last *Sefirah, malkhuth*, and the universal cosmos
that it contains) with their beginning (*kether*), as a flame is joined to
coal. For the Lord (the indivisible infinity of the *Sefiroth*) is One,
and has no second; and before the One (the only reality) what
canst thou count? . . . Ten *Sefiroth*, without anything (other
whatsoever); close thy mouth, that it may not speak (of the
Sefiroth, attributing mistaken aspects to them), and thy heart, that
it may not think (of the *Sefiroth* without being truly well-informed);
and if thy heart is carried away, come back to the place (of truth)
. . . Ten *Sefiroth*, without anything (other whatsoever): One
spirit alone of the living God, blessed be he, and may his name be
blessed, who lives for all eternity!'

5

One's study of the tenfold unity of the *Sefiroth* would remain incomplete without some mention of their particular role in regard to
the human being. This subject will be expanded in the chapter on
the 'Mystery of Man'. Let us here merely take note that the *Sefiroth* are simultaneously the archetypes of the inner being, both
spiritual and psychic, and of the outer or corporeal 'envelope' of
man. They are the causes and 'models' of all the intellectual lights
which spring up in his mind, of all the positive faculties and powers
of his soul, of all the principal organs and members of his body. In
the whole of creation there is no being which manifests the divine
qualities at the same time so synthetically and so explicitly as the
human being. The human being is to the cosmos what the *Sefiroth*
as a whole are to the ontological world. The Sefirothic entity is the
'figure' of God, man is his 'image'. All the *Sefiroth*, their essential
unity, their reciprocal relationships, as well as their cosmic manifestations, are reflected in the human being and in the interplay of
his multiple and hierarchical possibilities.

The Sefirothic unity contains the four worlds above and man
contains them below: the transcendental 'world of emanation' is
hidden in him, in his pure 'self', his divine essence; his supra-
individual and universal spirit is identified with the prototypical

'world of creation', whereas his individual soul, when it surpasses its illusory limits, is co-extensive with the subtle and celestial 'world of formation'; lastly, his corporeal 'quintessence', *avir*, the ether, is of such a nature that it can wholly embrace the sensory and terrestrial 'world of fact'.

From another side, each *Sefirah* can be regarded in its particular relationship with man. *Kether* is his pure and divine essence; *hokhmah*, his knowledge of God; *binah*, his ability to discriminate between the real and the unreal; *hesed*, his luminous nature which is always aspiring to the divine; *din*, his true judgement of all things; *tifereth*, his inner and outer beauty, his serenity, his love; *netsah*, his spiritual power; *hod*, his natural force; *yesod*, his activity; and *malkhuth*, his receptivity. In the same way, each *Sefirah* is the archetype of one of the principal organs or members of man, which is why the *Sefiroth* as a whole are called 'man on high' (*adam ilaah*), in whom *kether* is the 'hidden and superintelligible brain'; *hokhmah*, the 'right brain', which sees only the One; *binah*, the 'left brain', the principle of all distinction; *hesed*, the 'right' (or merciful) arm; *din*, the 'left' (or rigorous) arm; *tifereth*, the 'heart' or 'trunk', symbol of beauty and love; *netsah*, the 'right thigh', or cosmic positive force; *hod*, the 'left thigh' or cosmic negative force; *yesod*, the 'generative organ', or creative act; and *malkhuth*, the 'feet' or the 'female body', the end-place or 'substantial' recipient of the Sefirothic emanations. Lastly, from a special point of view, the 'ten fingers' also symbolize the Sefirothic decad.

All that is real in man, in his being, in his spirit, in his soul and in his body, is 'prefigured' and actualized by the *Sefiroth*. The nearer the 'lower man' comes spiritually to the Sefirothic unity, the nearer he comes to his own infinite 'figure', 'higher man', who is eternally one with God.

B. THE SEFIROTHIC HIERARCHY

I

Kether, the 'crown' – also called *kether elyon*, the 'supreme crown' amongst all the divine 'crowns', *Sefiroth*, or universal principles –

THE UNIVERSAL MEANING OF THE KABBALAH

is the uncreated and infinite all-reality of God. Nothing is outside of him; nothingness does not exist, for if it did it would no longer be nothingness but reality.

Kether, the only reality, on the one hand remains hidden in itself, in its absolute transcendence, and on the other manifests itself as uncreated immanence in the midst of its own transitory reflection: the creation.

Kether in itself is pure selfness, superintelligible essence, unity without trace of duality. It is reality without condition, without definition, in which God is what he is, beyond being; for Being is not the absolute reality as such, but its first affirmation.

Kether rests in its essence, its super-being – more than conscious of itself, without wishing anything whatsoever, without activity of any kind. For its essence is all; and, in it, all is it – all is all, without the slightest restriction, distinction, opposition or relation. In essence there is neither subject nor object, neither cause nor effect; there is only the One without a second, selfness without otherness, indivisible totality.

Kether, in its pure and absolute essence, has no aspects; it is the eternally mysterious reality: 'There is no other to be compared with it or associated with it' (*en sheni lehamshil lo lehahbirah*). It would be impossible to speak of it except by denying what it is not, or by placing it above all that is intelligible; that is, describing it in terms which are negative or superlative, or again, interrogatory.

Thus, the Kabbalah calls *kether* in itself: *ain*, 'nothingness', the absence of any definite or conditioned reality: non-being or super-being, non-cause, the absolute; *en sof*,[1] 'no end', infinite; *raza derazin*, 'mystery of mysteries', the superintelligible or super-conscious; *mi*, 'who?', the 'eternal object of search'; *attika deattikin*, the 'ancient of ancients', or principle of all universal principles; *attika kadisha*, the 'holy Ancient One', or supreme principle.

The absolute infinity of the supreme essence, the pure selfness of *kether*, excludes all otherness and consequently all knowledge

[1] Here the author conforms to the conventionally accepted transliteration of the words *ein sof* (infinite) according to its pronunciation: *en sof*.

of it: '*en sof* cannot be known, nor how it makes beginning or end . . .' What is the beginning? This is the supernal point, the beginning of all, hidden in 'thought' (a synonym of *hokhmah*, the supreme 'wisdom' which emanates from *kether*), and it makes the end (of all emanation) which is called 'the end of the matter' (Ecclesiastes 12:13). But beyond (in *kether*, pure infinity) there is 'no end', neither intention nor light nor lamp; all the lights are dependent on it (*kether*), but it cannot be reached. This is a supreme will, mysterious above all mysteries. It is 'nothingness' (*ain*, which is the absolute) (*Zohar, Pekude* 239a).

However, *kether* is not only the reality which excludes all that is not itself, but also the reality which is all-inclusive, since there is nothing outside of it. *Kether* is exclusive in so far as it is *ain*, the 'nothingness' of all that is not it; but as *en sof*, the infinite, it includes all that is possible in its boundless unity. Thus, although dwelling beyond being and knowledge in its non-causal essence, the only reality, thanks to its own unlimitedness, becomes conscious of its universal possibilities. Through its causal, intelligent and intelligible being, it knows itself and affirms itself as the unique, necessary ontological principle: 'I AM THAT I AM' (*Ehyeh asher Ehyeh*) (Exodus 3:14) 'I am the first and I am the last and beside me there is no God. And who, as I, can proclaim – let him declare it, and set it in order for me. . . . Is there a God beside me? Yea, there is no rock (necessary being beside me)' (Isaiah 44:6-8). 'Before me there was no God formed (manifested), neither shall any be after me. . . . I am God' (ibid. 43:10, 13).

In the absolute unity of its super-being (*ain*), *kether* bears no trace of multiplicity and transcends the causal unity of its being (*ehyeh*) which contains, in the entity of its intelligible aspects, or *Sefiroth*, the archetypes of the cosmic multitude: duality in principle. But at the same time the unity of being surpasses all dualism thanks to its infinity, which integrates itself – eternally and without any movement – in the pure and non-dual essence: super-being. In the One, therefore, there is no scission, no separation between being and super-being or non-being, nor is there any hierarchical confusion amongst them. Just as non-being includes, without distinction, being – of which it is the pure and indeterminate essence – but nevertheless is not being, having no need 'to be' in order to be real; so is it that being, while 'being' non-being, through essential identity with it, is nevertheless not non-being, in its first and ontological determination.

Kether is thus the principle which is identical at once with *ain* and with *ehyeh*, without nullifying the hierarchy of universal degrees; in other words, *kether* is *en sof* which, in its all-possibility, includes both being and non-being, while allowing each possibility to retain its own character. This is why one speaks of *kether* or *en sof* when considering this infinite, all-inclusive unity, but either of *ain* or of *ehyeh* when wishing to describe one or another of its two supreme aspects.

The identity of *kether* and *ain* is mysteriously revealed in the introduction to the Decalogue (Exodus 20:2) 'I (am) YHVH, thy God.' If the *ANY* are taken from the word *ANoKhY*, 'I', these letters – according to one application of the Kabbalistic permutation of letters – form by themselves the word AYN (nothingness); what remains is *Kh* (*kaf*), the initial of the word *kether*, which, according to the esoteric tradition, indicates that the *Sefirah kether* is the supreme universal degree, *ain*. Seen *ad intra*, *kether* therefore in no way differs from *ain*; it is only from the 'extrinsic' point of view of the emanated or manifested that it becomes *ehyeh*, the non-acting cause, situated between *ain*, the non-cause, and *hokhmah*, the divine 'wisdom', which is the first emanation and active cause.

In its aspect as *ehyeh*, or 'cause of causes', *kether* rests eternally and indistinctly in its absolute and unchangeable essence, *ain*; it does not act, but leaves it to the nine other *Sefiroth*, its emanations and ontological intellections, its 'lights' or 'lamps', to operate in its name. He who is *anokhi*, the divine 'I' or supreme 'self' of all things, remains unaffected by radiations and their cosmic effects. He contains all that is, as the unity within his unity; and each thing contains him in the deepest part of itself, as the One, the unchangeable. He is the essential identity of all things with the absolute. He is the absolute itself: the 'One without a second'.

Hokhmah, 'wisdom', or the first divine emanation, issues from the more than luminous 'nothingness' of *kether* as an infinitely radiant sun, whose innumerable, unbounded, undifferentiated sparks represent all the intelligible aspects, all the Sefirothic splendours, all that bears witness to the only truth.

Hokhmah is also called *mahshabah*, which signifies 'thought', 'meditation' and also 'art'. It is the radiation of the divine being, in which he contemplates himself, projecting or manifesting all things through the 'rays' emitted by his 'sparks'. Now the mystery of *hokhmah* is that each of its sparks, which are the essences or archetypes of all things, is but one with the divine being, the universal archetype: each of them is the infinite sun.

In *hokhmah*, God knows himself as being all that is, and all that is knows itself as God. There, no difference in being or in knowledge exists between him and one or another essence; for *hokhmah* is the eternal resolution of oppositions, the indifferentiation of every trace of duality, the ultimate meeting of extremes, the principial fusion – without hierarchical confusion – of all that is: 'Even the darkness is not dark for thee and the night shineth as the day: the darkness is even as light' (Psalms 139:12).

Hokhmah is both luminous and dark, intelligible and super-intelligible. It issues from the divine being, yet without issuing from it; in its infinity, it is hidden in *kether* – which is itself contained in *ain*, the absolute and superconscious self – while at the same time, in becoming conscious of all its knowable possibilities, it is as it were outside of *kether*. At its 'point of departure', *hokhmah* is therefore one with the 'mystery of mysteries', the incognizable; this being so, neither the way of its 'going out' from *kether* nor the way of its 're-entry' into *kether* can be defined.

'If that which is within the thought (*hokhmah*) cannot be comprehended, how much less the thought itself! What is within the thought no one can conceive, much less can one know *en sof* (or *kether*), of which no trace can be found and to which thought cannot reach by any means. But from the midst of the impenetrable mystery, from the first descent of *en sof* there glimmers a faint undiscernible light like the point of a needle, the hidden recess of thought, which even yet is not knowable until there extends from it a light in a place where there is some imprint of letters, (this "place" being identical with the prototypical "world of creation" and the "letters" synonymous with the cosmic archetypes) and from which they all issue' (*Zohar, Bereshith* 21a).

Hokhmah is called the 'father' (the active, determinant principle), or the 'father of fathers' (also the 'beginning', the first active cause, from which all the causal emanations proceed). The 'father' himself proceeds from the 'holy Ancient One' (*kether* or *ain*), as it is written in Job (28:12): 'And wisdom (*hokhmah*) comes out of *ain*.' (Literally: *me'ain*, i.e. whence?, a term by which the Kabbalah designates the indeterminate and inexpressible principle, the 'holy Ancient One'). As we have said, *kether*, as *ain* or super-being, is the absolute non-cause, and as *ehyeh* or being, the non-emanated and non-acting cause; it is only *hokhmah*, the first emanation, which acts by externalizing itself from *kether* as the sun emerges from night.

Hokhmah, divine thought, is the intelligible and indistinct essence of all the *Sefiroth* which proceed from it and of all the cosmic reflections of these. By 'thinking' and 'meditating', God simultaneously projects and resolves his thought and all its content; but where he does not 'think' – at the eternal 'end of thought' in *ain*, his non-determination and non-knowledge or superconsciousness – there are no creatures and no archetypes: this is the 'nothingness' of all that is not he. It is also said that 'the beginning and the end (of everything emanated) is contained in divine thought. . . .' When this thought is manifested, it is named the 'father of fathers', and everything is enclosed in that alone, as it is written (Psalms 104:24): 'In wisdom hast thou made them all'. And the *Zohar* (*Terumah* 155a) also says: 'God created man in the mystery of wisdom (*hokhmah*, which is his intelligent and intelligible essence) and fashioned him with great art and breathed into him the breath of life, so that he might know and comprehend the mysteries of wisdom to apprehend the glory (or real presence) of his Lord.'

The essential mystery of *hokhmah* is the One: it knows only the One and all in the One. This is why it is called beatitude or the eternal 'Eden', the 'Tree of Life', the 'first (and uncreated) Tables of the Torah', of which the 'transparent stones sparkling with light make up that unity in which there is no division'. It is beyond the distinction between good and evil, beyond the 'relationships' between one reality and another; in it, all that is is infinite within the infinite. For this reason, when contemplating *hokhmah*, all manifested things have to be transposed ideally into their supreme archetype. Everything being thus re-integrated in its first perfection, its divine aspect, its infinity, all becomes one in the One; and for the spirit of man the One becomes the only truth.

3

Before manifesting itself to the worlds, the divine being reveals itself, in its wisdom, its act of pure knowledge, to itself, that is, to its own receptivity, its 'intelligence': *binah*. *Binah* dwells in the luminous plenitude of *hokhmah*, like the emptiness or darkness of a hidden mirror; and it comes out from this light and envelops it, becoming its supreme plane of reflection, at the moment when the light issues from the more than luminous darkness of essence. Thus *hokhmah* pours out all the intelligible possibilities of *kether* into the midst of *binah* in a single undifferentiated emanation. The infinite radiation from the face of God enters the void of his boundless receptivity, into the face of his supreme 'mirror': *binah*. The luminous and beatific flow of *hokhmah* travels from the face of *kether* to the face of *binah*, which – eternally and without any movement – reflects and projects it, as it is received, back into *kether*. But this is only to express in symbolic terms that *kether*, *hokhmah* and *binah* are the one and only God revealing himself to himself: 'The Ancient One, seen face to face . . . who cannot be defined except as the unity' of the self-subsistent Being and of the knowledge which knows itself through itself.

'The first three *Sefiroth*: "Crown", "Wisdom" and "Intelligence" have to be considered as one and the same reality. (They

THE UNIVERSAL MEANING OF THE KABBALAH

are identical by essential fusion, without hierarchical confusion.)
The first (*kether*) represents knowledge or knowing (divine consciousness in itself); the second (*hokhmah*) represents that which
knows (the active or determinant principle of knowledge); and
the third (*binah*) represents that which is known (the receptive
and reflective aspect of knowledge). In order to make clear to
oneself this (ontological and cognitive) identity, one must remember that the Creator's knowing (his consciousness or knowledge)
is not like that of his creatures; for in creatures the knowing is
distinct from the subject and is brought to bear on objects which
are likewise distinct from the subject. This is expressed by the
three terms: thought, that which thinks, and that which is thought.
On the contrary, the Creator is himself knowledge, that which
knows, and that which is known all at the same time. His way of
knowing does not consist of applying his thought to things outside
himself; by knowing himself and perceiving himself, he knows
and perceives all that is. Nothing exists that is not united with him
and which he does not find in his own essence' (Moses Cordovero:
Pardes Rimmonim, 'Garden of Pomegranates'.).

This is also the meaning of the statement in the Kabbalah:
'The holy Ancient One exists with three heads (or principial
aspects: *kether, hokhmah, binah*), which form only one (ontological reality)'; or again: 'everything is in them; all the mysteries
are contained in them; (and) they themselves are contained in the
holy One, the Ancient of Ancients: in him, all is enclosed; he contains all.' Inasmuch as the face of the supreme mirror, *binah*, is
turned towards the face of pure being, *kether*, it forms but one
'great face' with it and with its radiation, *hokhmah*: the transcendental 'great face' (*arikh anpin*)[1] of God, who embraces being and
super-being in his infinity. However, *hokhmah*, God's wisdom, is

---

[1] *Arikh anpin*, an Aramaic term of the Zohar, means literally 'long face'
or, if taken as synonymous with the Hebrew *erekh apaim*, it means the 'long-
animous' (cf. Exodus 34:6). *Arikh anpin* strictly denotes *kether*; but if one con-
siders that *kether* or the holy Ancient One exists with three heads which form
only one, it is the whole supreme Tri-Unity which becomes identified, by
extension, with the *arikh anpin*.

not only his eternal becoming conscious of his own transcendent unity, but also his universal will, by which he wishes to reveal his immanent reflections to his being and his being to his reflections or cosmic effects. Thus, *hokhmah*, the supreme clarity – being too dazzling to be revealed to the worlds directly – is wrapped in the uncreated 'veil' or universal emptiness of *binah*, the revelatory and creative 'intelligence'. Through *binah* this clarity which in itself is hidden in the darkness of the absolute, appears as intelligible light or divine spirit. Indeed, the clarity of the 'great face' is so sublime that it unites with the superintelligible itself and is called 'who?' (*mi*): which is beyond the grasp of distinctive intellection and constitutes the 'eternal object of (spiritual) search'. *Binah*, in its function of universal 'mother', discerns all the 'sparks' or 'seeds' of the created, all manifestable possibilities, in the midst of the undifferentiated and dazzling light of the 'father'. In this purely causal and eternal act, *binah* is like a prism or mirror, broken into a myriad of 'facets' each one of which reflects the divine 'great face' in its own way, as well as the content of every other facet. In this way, God contemplates himself in *binah*, the universal 'mother', as the One in the multiple, and sees at the same time all the 'shattered fragments' of his mirror, all his innumerable aspects, joined together again in the undifferentiated unity of *hokhmah*, the transcendent 'father'.

While *hokhmah*, ontological wisdom, only determines the pure being of all things – that being which is one, indistinct and infinite – on the other hand, *binah*, onto-cosmological 'intelligence', determines their pure quality, their particular aspect of divinity, their own archetype; and *binah* synthesizes all these archetypes in the seven '*Sefiroth* of (cosmic) construction' which emanate from it and are the immediate causes of the creation. Thus the manifestable possibilities of the divine being do not pass directly from *hokhmah* into the cosmogonic act, but are first discerned and qualitatively determined by *binah*, and 'channelled' thereafter through the seven cosmological principles until they enter the created 'ocean'.

Let it be made clear, however, that the determination of the first qualities by *binah* is not to be confused with any discrimination such as can be exercised by a created being; for in *binah* there is neither multitude nor effective diversity: it is multitude in eternal and essential fusion with the undifferentiated unity of *hokhmah*. This is why the *Zohar* says that *binah* issues from *kether* with *hokhmah* and that they remain together; that they are never separated from each other; that they never leave one another, as it is written in Genesis (2:10): '(only) one river went out of Eden (*kether*).' Thus *binah* is the principle of all distinction although without itself including any effective distinction: 'Although the supreme mother is by no means rigorous, yet rigour emanates from her.' *Binah* is unity in multitude and the multitude finds unity in her.

'In the mother (*binah*), (unitive) benevolence never comes to an end'; she is the supreme *yobel* (Jubilee), the stage of final deliverance. In other words, the earthly *yobel*, or 'year of the Jubilee', symbolizes *binah*, liberation from everything manifested; for during that year all the slaves are set free, all things revert in full to their original owners, all debts are cancelled, no work is done in the fields and the vineyards. 'Ye shall hallow the fiftieth year and proclaim liberty throughout the land for all its inhabitants. It shall be a Jubilee (*yobel*) unto you' (Leviticus 25:10). *Binah* is also called the 'place of the breaking of vows' – which means above all the degree where all traces of the cosmos are erased – and also the 'place of penitence' and of 'atonements', the purification and liberation from all sins, including that of the illusion of existence outside of God. It is in his power to free servants, to free all men, to free the guilty, to purify everything; as it is written (*ibid.* 16:30): 'For on this day (the Day of atonement, one of the symbols of *binah*), shall atonement be made for you, to cleanse you; from all your sins shall ye be clean before YHVH.'

4

When *arikh anpin*, the transcendental 'great face' of *kether-hokhmah-binah*, turns towards the possibility of creation, it wraps itself in the sevenfold 'veil' of the '*Sefiroth* of construction' and appears through it as *zeir anpin*,[1] the 'small face', or principle of immanence; for the finite is unable to bear direct contact with the supreme.

The 'features' or aspects of the 'small face' of God are no longer inaccessible, like those of the 'great face', but come within the reach of manifested spirit as the direct archetypes of created things. This is why the 'small face' is called *eleh*, 'these' – intelligible and analogical determination – whereas the 'great face' is designated by the interrogation *mi*, 'Who?', the supreme determination beyond intelligibility and analogy, essentially identical with the indeterminate, the inexpressible. But in reality the two divine faces are one: the only God looks at himself, both 'without a veil', as *arikh anpin*, and 'through the veil', when appearing to himself and to created beings as *zeir anpin*. The 'small face' depends on the holy Ancient One (*kether* in so far as it includes *hokhmah* and *binah*) and is one with it. The 'small' and the 'great face' of God together are the causal unity of all the archetypes of *Sefiroth*, known as *elohim*, 'gods': '*Eleh* (the "small face") added to *mi* (the "great face" which is turned towards the created as *im*) formed (*eleh+im=*) *elohim*.' It is in the light of this truth that the exhortation of Isaiah (40:26) is to be understood: 'Lift up your eyes on high and see: Who (*mi*) hath created (caused) these (*eleh*)?'

The first 'feature' which appears on the 'small face' of God is *hesed*, his 'grace'. '*Hesed* comes from the side of the "father" (*hokhmah*)' qualitatively, but hierarchically from the side of the 'mother', *binah*. *Hokhmah*, as the infinite and indistinct flow of pure beatitude, remains what it is only in the midst of the supreme tri-unity, in which it travels – symbolically speaking – from divine face to divine face, without being in any way modified. When it

---

[1] *Zeir anpin* is an Aramaic term of the Zohar which literally means 'short face' or, if considered synonymous with the Hebrew *ketsar apaim*, it means 'the impatient' (cf. Prov. 14:17). It designates, strictly speaking, the six active *Sefiroth* of construction, which manifest through the receptive *sefirah*, *malkhuth*, divine immanence.

issues from the 'great face' in order to engender the creative radiation of the 'small face', its clarity is 'broken down' by the 'prism' of the supreme 'intelligence' into seven Sefirothic lights, which, however, remain inseparable in their 'co-infinity' as in their co-operation. Without this extrinsic refraction of the eternal and unlimited clarity, creation, which by definition is limited, could not be effected; there would be no cosmic effects, nothing but the transcendent reality of the 'great face'.

Hesed, 'grace', the first cosmological radiation of God, is not, therefore, beatitude reposing in itself, but that 'sacred happiness' which is given to 'others' and according to the need of the 'other'. It is charity in every possible sense of the word, the unlimitedness of the Creator in so far as it realizes and, with boundless kindness, adapts to the limits of the created being. This is necessary being which gives its reality in the form of life to everything that has to exist, and which delivers all things from existential limitations.

These gifts of grace would be impossible were it not for the simultaneous determination of the cosmic limits and conditions, for if there were no limits there would be nothing but infinity, beatitude in itself. In order to be able to reveal itself in its manifestable possibilities, grace is obliged to restrict them: this it does by means of rigour or universal 'judgement', *din*, which it inherited from the supreme discernment, *binah*, and which it keeps enclosed in the midst of its luminosity, like a dark seed. When this seed develops, it takes on the aspect of a special *Sefirah*, which appears to contradict, but in reality completes that from which it issues.

Hokhmah determines the being of the archetypes, *binah* their quality; *hesed* manifests their unity and unlimitedness, *din* 'measures' their differentiated manifestations and thereby fixes the fundamental conditions or limitations of all that exists. Thus *din* manifests as the universal law, determining the order of cosmic nature, so that the latter may receive *hesed*, the grace or supernatural, uncreated and infinite immanence of God.

Grace is called the 'right arm' of God and the law his 'left arm'. Thanks to these two opposite but complementary manifestations,

God keeps all creation in balance. The Creation indeed could not exist through grace alone, nor through his rigour alone. For *hesed*, grace, is the continuous emanation of the infinite which could have no relation with the limited cosmos were it not previously penetrated by the cause of all limitation: *din*, the discontinuous emanation or judgement of God. If, on the other hand, universal judgement ceased to be penetrated by grace, the creative act would become impossible; for then there would be nothing but the negation of all negation of the infinite, that is, the annihilation of everything finite.

Without the affirmative power of grace, which is none other than the creative, conservative and redemptive presence of God in the midst of the cosmos, nature could bring nothing to birth. Fixed within their limits by God's rigour, all things participate intimately, in their positive reality, in his immanent grace. Grace is the pure affirmation of his transcendence; the luminous 'ray' linking all the cosmic effects to their supreme cause; the universal 'axis' around which gravitate all the worlds, all beings, all things.

Hesed is God's love, which created the world in preceding his rigour, *din*. God in himself is pure beatitude, and when he leans over the possibility of his creation, his bliss becomes 'kindness of kindnesses', goodness, mercy, that is, grace. In God, rigour is not anger, but an indistinct aspect of his truth, which, in turn, differs in no way from bliss. For his truth is that he alone is; and his one an universal reality is his beatitude.

God created the world by means of his truth and his bliss at the same time. He created it in order to affirm – by his grace, manifesting his truth as bliss – that all is in him, and in order to deny – by his rigour, glorifying his reality as uniqueness – all that, in an illusory way, is 'outside of him'.

Rigour, the negation of the negation of the only reality, is first manifested as the void or cosmic darkness, excluding all distinct creation before the 'One without a second'. But grace, or the direct affirmation of divine infinity – which includes, penetrates and integrates all limits – prevails over the exclusive action of rigour and fills the dark, cosmic emptiness with the luminous,

47

spiritual fullness of its immanence, thus engendering all created beings and things. Rigour is transformed then into a 'recipient' of grace and takes on the appearance, in the differentiated creation, of the 'measure' of the existential limits, from their prime definition until their final extinction in the infinite. Grace, by virtue of its unlimitedness, expands the created being indefinitely to the fullness of its measure, while existential conditions continue to be actuated by rigour; but where the cosmic measure comes close to its end, rigour, in extreme contraction, causes the totality of created being to return into its first origin, which is the 'grace of graces', the infinite bliss of the only truth, the only reality.

And so one sees, more precisely, why divine rigour – which after all tends only to dissolve everything created which, by its own natural limitations, is opposed to infinite grace – could not be identified with God's anger alone. His anger in fact is no more than a cosmic aspect of his rigour. *Din* becomes anger only in the eyes of and in the midst of created beings and solely to the extent that created beings glorify themselves as 'another God' and deny God's 'only reality'. Where the created is but the pure and direct expression of the creative will of God, it cannot be the object of his wrath; it is then, on the contrary, the receptacle of his grace, which fills it with uncreated and blissful light and finally reabsorbs it into itself.

God's rigour denies all that is not God, the only reality; it negates nothingness, which, thanks to God's infinite all-reality, does not exist. But for that to be so, God himself is obliged to lend a kind of unreal reality, the deceptive semblance of something 'other than him' to non-existent nothingness; this is the existential illusion, and is effected by *binah*, God's onto-cosmological intelligence, which is nothing other than his receptivity or void, his dark possibility, unintelligible and antinomic, hidden within his luminous fullness, which is one and unitive, that is, in *hokhmah*. Thus *binah* appears to be the deepest cause of 'evil'; yet it would be wrong to think that there could be the least trace of any sort of evil in God, the one good, for in him there is no trace of any limit. *Binah* determines 'evil' but simultaneously negates it by means of the 'good' opposed to it: *binah* affirms the good through *hesed* and negates evil through *din*. In creating the world, God separates it from himself by his rigour, only to unite it with himself by his grace. In fact, rigour not only separates the creation from the creator, as well as all created worlds, beings and things from one another, but finally it also separates them from existential separativity in conjunction with the redemptive act of grace, which unites them all with the One.

Rigour, therefore, is only grace in so far as grace appears negative in manifestation; it is the negation of the negation of reality, hence the affirmation of reality, its grace. And, as we have seen, grace would not be affirmative without its negative possibility, rigour. This is why the Kabbalah says: 'Where there is rigour, there is also grace, and where there is grace, there is also rigour.' Grace and rigour are essentially one, that One who rules over all things and who, according to the *Zohar* (*Beshallah* 51b), is comparable to '. . . a king who combines in himself the balance and harmony of all attributes, and therefore his countenance always shines like the sun and he is serene because of his wholeness and perfection; but when he judges, he can condemn as well as acquit. A fool, seeing that the king's countenance is bright, thinks that there is nothing to be afraid of; but a wise man says to himself, "Although the king's countenance shines, it is because he is perfect and combines benevolence with justice. In that brightness judgement is hidden, and therefore I must be careful."' The Holy One is such a king. Rabbi Judah found this idea expressed in the words (Malachi 3:6): 'For I, YHVH, change not'; it is as though God were saying: 'In me, all attributes are joined together in harmony; in me, the two aspects, grace and rigour, are but one'.

5

Tifereth, God's 'beauty', is his infinite unity in so far as it is revealed as the plenitude and blissful harmony of all his possibilities. Whereas in *kether* these dwell within their supreme identity, in *tifereth* they appear as so many particular archetypes, each of which connects with the others by essential fusion and qualitative interpenetration. This is why the Kabbalah says: 'When the colours (or qualities of the principle) are intermingled, he is called *tifereth*.'

The archetypes are at first pure and indistinct lights, which only receive their 'colours' or specific qualities in *din*, the supreme 'judgement'; and it is in *tifereth*, beauty emanating from judgement, that these divine colours intermingle in perfect harmony. For *tifereth* is above all others the mediatory *Sefirah*, God's 'heart' or 'compassion' (*rahamim*), which embraces and fuses everything which is 'above' and 'below', 'on the right' or 'on the left' in the world of emanation. It is called the 'sun' or the supreme 'wheel', because its unlimited rays connect all the *Sefiroth* and synthesize their antinomies in its one centre or 'hub'. In this unitive aspect, God's beauty is like his grace, *hesed*, and also like his supreme tri-unity, *kether–hokhmah–binah*. Yet it is different from them in that their indistinct possibilities appear in *tifereth* as the definite and rigorous 'measures' of all things. In *tifereth* the archetypes – issuing from the 'darkness' of judgement – are revealed in their principal 'forms' or 'colours'; and in it alone is actualized – eternally and without any movement – the interpenetration of these supra-formal 'forms': their fusion into one single infinite 'form', filled with an ocean of divinely coloured light.

In other words, in God's beauty all his causal possibilities appear as the perfected 'models' of created things and these, even under the most contradictory aspects; in it, God 'carves his (eternal) sculptures' to the last degree of precision and with a perfect art which brings all the contrasts together into a supreme concordance. In God's beauty all his aspects are what they are, in all their relationships and in all their reciprocity; in God's beauty each *Sefirah* opens up into its own whole fullness and magnificence, penetrating and penetrated by the other *Sefiroth*. For this reason, *tifereth* is called *da'ath*, divine 'knowing', the omniscience or total consciousness of God, of which it is written (Proverbs 24:4): 'and by *da'ath* the rooms (or spiritual "receptivities") are filled with all precious and pleasant (Sephirothic) riches (which are "precious" in the cognitive aspect and "pleasant" in their harmony).'

Divine beauty is at the same time: more-than-luminous darkness; dazzling plenitude of being; boundless void, pure receptive power; immeasurable grace; the rigorous measure of all things; love and peace, uniting everything with everything; life, joy and freedom; the disappearance of all boundaries in the infinite; the act of redemption; majesty. All these aspects, which are simply a description of the ten *Sefiroth*, interpenetrate one another and form the unlimited expressions of the 'small face', revealing the mysteries and lights of the 'great face' enclosed within it. For *tifereth*, by itself, is the whole of the 'small face'; it is the 'king' or the 'son' which constitutes the synthesis of all the divine emanations, both of those from which it issues and of those which issue from it: all appear as its own aspects.[1] 'The son takes possession of all (which emanates from *kether*), inherits every (particular archetype) and expands (through his central and universal radiation) over all.'

The essential principle of divine beauty is the identity of the absolute (*ain*) – which excludes all that is not itself – and of the infinite (*en sof*) – which includes all that is real; it is the unity of the more than luminous darkness of non-being with the dazzling plenitude of pure being, the supreme and most mysterious of unities, which is revealed in the saying (Song of Songs 1:5): 'I am black, but comely . . .' This essential principle of divine beauty, from which radiate both the pure truth of the only reality, eclipsing all that is not it, and at the same time unlimited bliss in which each thing swims as though in a shoreless ocean, is nothing other than *kether*, which encloses all the polar aspects of God, eternally and without distinction. When *kether* reveals itself, its infinite and unitive aspect is expressed by *hokhmah* and by *hesed*, while its absolute or exclusive character is manifested by *binah* and by *din*. These two kinds of antinomic emanations are indispensable in view of creation; we have seen how, in order to create, both

[1] See Figs. III and IV of the diagrams on p. 29.

rigorous truth and generous bliss are necessary; or, in other words, measure in all things, judgement of their qualities, universal law on the one hand and on the other the unlimitedness of grace, giving rise to all life, joy and freedom. And in order that these two opposites, in which are concentrated, in one way or another, all the divine aspects, may be able to produce the cosmos, there has to be, not only absolute identity 'above' between these two, but also their interpenetration and existential fusion 'below'. This fusion or synthesis of all the revealed antinomies of God, which can be summed up in the two general terms 'grace' and 'rigour', takes place in *tifereth*, 'beauty'. In *tifereth*, the rigorous truth which God alone is, differs in no way from his mercy which unites everything with him. In God's 'heart', the eternal measure of things is as though dissolved in the incommensurability of his redemptive grace. When divine beauty is manifested, grace crystallizes mysteriously in the created 'measures' or forms and radiates through them, leaving the imprint of its author on the work of creation.

The love of God which, as it operates in the universe, is at the same time radiation from and attraction to his beauty, creates the world according to the principle of the harmony of his causal possibilities. This harmony, *tifereth*, determines the principial or ideal form of the cosmos. This form is purely spiritual or supra-formal: the 'world of (prototypical) creation' (*olam haberiyah*), which can be called the 'sphere of which the centre is everywhere and the circumference nowhere',[1] since the *shekhinah*, infinite omnipresence, dwells in it alone. The spherical form is what expresses plenitude and harmony and characterizes beauty; it must, however, be pointed out that this has no longer anything to do with the simple sphere having only one centre, in conformity with order in space, since in the midst of the principial form every 'point' grouped around the centre is simultaneously and mysteriously the centre itself: here also there is but one centre, but each

---

[1] In other words, the true subject of this phrase used by Pascal is the spiritual world.

'point' in this sphere is a spiritual archetype, an immanent aspect of God which is one with his omnipresence; and in each 'centre' which is identical with the divine centre, all the 'centres' are reflected in their specific 'colours': there is interpenetration, fusion without confusion, omnipresence of all the archetypes. From this plenitude or immanent beauty of the One proceed all created forms, in their pristine beauty and perfection.

A thing is beautiful and perfect when it manifests, in one harmonious mode or another, the fullness of the possibilities of its kind, and when that kind reveals, in one way or another, a spiritual archetype or divine aspect in all its purity. Now, since every aspect of the One contains and expresses, in its own way, all his aspects, every perfect manifestation of a 'deiform' species reveals in the light of its own quality, the plenitude of causal possibilities, namely universal and divine beauty. A thing is ugly if it participates only imperfectly in its pure archetype, or if its species is not in conformity with divine perfection. On the level of man – the most complex of creatures, in his constitution and possibilities of transformation – this truth has to be understood in its particular application, taking into account the respective aspects of 'inner' and 'outer' beauty. In the case of non-human species, the outer aspect reveals the inner quality of the being or thing, and this by reason of their passive nature which excludes existential dualism. In the case of the human species, endowed with reason, free will and a conscious relationship with the divine spirit, the outer or corporeal aspect of a being may express a certain static result of his personal development, actualized in the course of 'previous lives', whereas the inner aspect – whether psychic or spiritual – may be transformed, in one direction or the other, in the course of this life, either by virtues and knowledge, or on the contrary by their absence. Indeed, a man may be born ugly, from the physical point of view, whereas his soul may display ethical and spiritual beauty during this life: and in this case it is possible that the inner beauty may eclipse to a great extent his bodily ugliness. On the other hand, there are men with outer beauty – resulting from 'previous merits' – whose soul becomes corrupt in this life; then the inner ugliness finally becomes visible and the bodily beauty becomes more or less illusory.

The human being is truly beautiful when the generosity of grace in him is expressed in the harmonious measure of forms; when the darkness of his limitations is effaced by the light of the infinite springing up from the depths of his being; when the spirit penetrates his substance and reveals, in one way or another, the blissful fullness of the One.

6

The supreme or 'essential' tri-unity, *kether–hokhmah–binah*, is revealed by the creative triad, *hesed–din–tifereth*, and the latter is manifested by its threefold executive power: *netsah–hod–yesod*. This universal power is made up of an emanation of grace and an emanation of rigour, and by the creative, conservative and destructive act, which synthesizes them and of which they represent the antinomic and complementary aspects.

The emanation of grace is the *Sefirah netsah*, divine 'victory'; this is the 'male', active and positive power of the creator, which produces all the manifested worlds in giving life to all beings and things by 'extension, multiplication and force'. Thanks to *netsah*, the transcendent beauty of God, *tifereth*, is spread over the whole of creation. *Netsah* issues from *tifereth* as an infinite flow of pure life, made of light and bliss, with which it fills everything born from the illusory or cosmic 'multiplication' of the One.

The multiplication itself does not come from *netsah*, but from the emanation opposed and complementary to it, that is, from *hod*, divine 'glory'. *Hod* springs forth at first with *netsah* from *tifereth*, in a single indistinct effusion; this first effusion is what is called *netsah*, whereas the distinct emanation emerging from it is *hod*, the 'female', receptive and negative power of the creator, that which separates, forms and transforms all the worlds produced indifferently by *netsah*. The 'glory' of God emerges from his 'victory', in order to project the apparent multiplicity of the One in the cosmic milieu and in order to reabsorb this apparency into the One.

Such is the nature of the two attributes or powers of God's eternal act; this creative and destructive act is in itself a specific archetype, namely, *yesod*, the 'foundation' of cosmic existence. The *Zohar* says that the union of the light and active emanation, *netsah* – which comes from the 'right' or positive side of the Sefirothic tree – with the dark and receptive emanation *hod* – on the 'left' or negative side – is what causes the ninth *Sefirah*, *yesod*, to appear, this being the 'basis' of the created world; and when, united in *yesod* – which dwells in the 'middle pillar' – the 'male' light *netsah* fills the darkness or 'emptiness' of its 'female', *hod* with the 'excess' of its creative overflowing, then cosmic equilibrium is established.

Yesod is the eternal and immutable balance between the 'full' and expansive emanation of *netsah* and the 'empty' and restrictive emanation of *hod*, or between the manifestation and reabsorption of all things; *yesod* is the unique act, which simultaneously reveals and reintegrates all that is emanated and manifested; this is why it is also called *kol*, the 'all'. Indeed, all the *Sefiroth* 'emerge' from the divine essence and 'return' into it together with all their cosmic manifestations in one single 'eternal moment'; therefore they can be said to emerge without emerging and that there is neither emanation nor manifestation except from the subjective and relative point of view of manifested beings, whereas, from the objective and principial point of view of the pure and universal being, none of his aspects has ever emerged from him, just as, from the superintelligible 'point of view' of the supreme and non-dual essence, which transcends subjectivity and objectivity alike, there is absolutely nothing, not even any non-emanated aspect, which can be associated in any way whatsoever with his one and only selfness.

In the face of the 'One without a second', creation, this semblance of a 'second' could not really exist. It is only from our ephemeral point of view that there is a creation. But if creation exists only 'non-existentially', such non-existence nevertheless cannot be nothingness, purely and simply; it is the 'great illusion' woven out of myriads of fleeting shadows of which we are the witnesses. This deceptive mirage of the cosmos, this vast phantas-magoria, with all its worlds, its beings and its things, is produced by the unreal 'multiplication' of the One. *Netsah*, the full and continuous flow of manifestable possibilities – a flow which never 'dries up', in its circuit carrying all things from the One to the One – fills its 'receptacle', *hod*; and the emptiness of *hod* coats and separates each 'spark' hidden in the luminous and undifferentiated influx of *netsah*. Then *netsah* penetrates the interruptions produced by *hod* with its uninterrupted emanation and thus ensures the causal concatenation of all these illusorily separated possibilities. Thanks to this continuity[1] in the manifestation of things – main-tained throughout all the cosmic separations – there is a logical sequence of reflections or 'images' of God, the multitude of which is finally reintegrated in his unity.

Let us add that *netsah* and *hod* represent in particular the sources of prophetic revelation. God's 'thought' is first expressed by his uncreated word, *tifereth*, of which *netsah* is the effusion of pure and spiritual light; *hod* is the refraction and reverberation of this light and *yesod* is its descent into receptive substance. In other words, *netsah* receives the light of *tifereth* and *hod* gives it the semblance of multiple and sacred forms, which *yesod*[2] inspires into man through the intermediary of the last *Sefirah*, *malkhuth*, the real presence of God.

7

The supreme and mysterious tri-unity, called *mi* ('who?', the superintelligible), is the 'real subject of (spiritual) enquiry; but after a man, by means of enquiry and reflection, has reached the

---

[1] Let us remember that *netsah* can be translated either as 'victory' or as 'constancy', 'continuity' or 'perpetuity'.

[2] *Yesod* is also called *tsedek*, 'justice', because it manifests its two antinomic aspects, *netsah* and *hod*, in perfect complementarity; all the grace and all the rigour appearing in the creation express nothing but God's justice and actu-alize universal equilibrium.

utmost limit of knowledge, he (comes down again and) stops at *mah* ("what?" [the unintelligible]), as if to say, "What" knowest thou? "What" have thy searchings achieved? Everything is as baffling as the beginning' (*Zohar* 1, 1b). Before, during and after all spiritual investigation, man finds himself face to face with one and the same mystery: the 'One without a second'. But the mystery is a mystery solely for the reason that there is 'otherness'; it is this, the creature, which hides the divine unity and asks the question: 'who' and 'what' am I? Without this 'otherness' there is neither 'who' nor 'what', neither search nor mystery: there is nothing but the only reality in its non-dual and absolute selfness.

Therefore it is the existence of a 'second' in the midst of the 'One without a second' which makes the only reality mysterious; in the end, all spiritual search comes to the question: by virtue of 'what' (*mah*) does cosmic existence become concrete? The Kabbalah answers: this 'what', *mah*, is divine immanence, the last *Sefirah*, *malkhuth*, the 'kingdom' of God, which produces, encircles and penetrates the whole of creation. *Malkhuth*, situated at the lower extremity of the 'middle pillar', is not only the 'recipient' of all the emanations of the *Sefiroth* on the luminous or intelligible 'right side', and on the dark or unintelligible 'left side', but also of the central *Sefiroth*, the highest of which is *kether*, the superintelligible principle. In other words, *malkhuth* is the 'descent', the *shekhinah* or omnipresence of the supreme, which is manifested on the one side by intelligible emanations united in the universal spirit and on the other by unintelligible emanations, the darkness of which becomes concrete in creative substance. So *malkhuth* has an essential aspect, a spiritual aspect and a substantial aspect; in its essence it is superintelligible and identical with the 'who?' (*mi*); it is the 'end which comes to join the beginning' and, through that, the 'cause of causes', which is unknowable; in its spirituality, it is intelligible: it is the 'light of the world', called 'that' (*eleh*); and in its substantiality, it is unintelligible: it is the 'firmament which has no light from itself', the 'what?' (*mah*) of all substance.

Now, although *malkhuth* is equally the presence of *mi* and of *eleh*, it is called *mah*, because it is by itself a purely receptive and unintelligible principle, an empty 'mirror' which simply reflects all that is 'above', in the divine world, and 'below', in creation. It manifests nothing which is not strictly in conformity with the 'intentions of the (divine) king'; this is why 'all the powers of the king are conferred upon it', and why it is the 'perfect mediator at the king's side'. As we have just said, it is not only the faithful 'witness' of every transcendental emanation, but also of every cosmic manifestation, and it is *malkhuth* which attracts all grace and rigour to the world: for '*mah* will be your equal: it will show on high the very attitude you will adopt below'.

As passive and receptive principle, the end-point of the influx of all the emanations of the *Sefiroth*, *malkhuth* is called the 'woman' or the 'wife', the 'queen' of the divine 'king'. As the generative cause, manifesting by cosmic reproduction all that she has 'inherited' from the 'father', from the 'supreme mother' and from the 'son', she is called the 'lower mother'; and in the aspect of un-created substance, 'pure and incomprehensible', she is called the 'daughter' and 'virgin of Israel'. Finally, inasmuch as she manifests, in the midst of the cosmos, the unity of the divine emanations – or certain of their aspects – of which she then represents the descent or direct revelation, she is called *shekhinah*, the 'imma-nence' or real presence of God; and, when the immanence takes the form of the mystical body of Israel, she bears the name 'community of Israel'.

Malkhuth, the 'lower mother', is from the cosmological point of view what *binah*, the 'highest mother', is from the ontological point of view; like the latter, she is on the one hand the 'mirror' and on the other the 'prism' of divine emanation. On the one side she sends back to the 'king', *tifereth*, all the radiation she receives from him through the intermediary of his act, *yesod*; and she is thus eternally united with him, her 'husband', who in turn is infinitely united with the 'supreme crown', *kether elyon*. On the other side she projects the influx of the 'king' out from the causal or Sefi-rothic unity and thereby creates the cosmos; and in her cosmic manifestation she herself 'descends', as immanence, into the created being in order to connect him with his transcendental source.

However, in considering these attributes and principal modes of activity of *malkhuth*, we have not yet answered the question as to what it is as substance. Now it is not a distinct substance, but rather the undifferentiated, uncreated principle of all substance which in no way emerges from the infinite and indivisible unity of the creative causes: this principle envelopes them and is yet hidden within them, like 'very pure and imperceptible air'. What is this 'air' which is not breathable in the same way as the air which surrounds us? It is *avir*, the universal 'ether', the quintessence of the four subtle or celestial elements and of the four corporeal or terrestrial elements. And what is the ether itself? It is none other than the infinite receptivity of the divine 'intelligence': *binah*. 'The father (*hokhmah*) is the spirit hidden in the "Ancient of days" (*kether*) in whom this "very pure air" (identical with *binah*) is enclosed.' The universal ether envelopes the intelligible emanation of *hokhmah* from the moment of its first emergence from the 'ancient of days': 'it unites with the (spiritual) flame issuing from the (supreme) and brilliant lamp' and follows it in the whole course of its descent towards cosmic possibility and throughout the cosmos itself.

'Above', the ether is the infinite receptivity of *binah*, by virtue of which God reveals himself to himself; 'below', it is the cosmic receptivity of *malkhuth*, which becomes concrete in creative substance. In other words, that which is pure receptivity in *binah* and creative contraction in *din* becomes cosmic emptiness in *hod* and finally undifferentiated and causal substance in *malkhuth*. This process of principial 'substantialization' has its positive point of departure in *hokhmah*, whose luminous plenitude is manifested by *hesed*, and which, having received its universal form from *tifereth*, is manifested by *netsah* as the 'life of the worlds', which *yesod* communicates to *malkhuth*, the substance.

In this way, all the *Sefiroth* 'descend' from *kether*, in perfect co-emanation and co-operation, and are finally concentrated in *malkhuth* and manifested by *malkhuth* in the cosmic mode.

However, as we have seen, if one wishes to remain close to pure and superintelligible truth, there can be no question of anything having emanated or being distinct from the supreme, the only reality, the 'One without a second'.

III Creation, the Image of God

Lift up your eyes on high   and see who hath created these?
Isaiah 40:26

I

The principal aim of tradition in regard to the forms and laws of
the cosmos is to connect all things with their first and divine cause
and thus show man their true meaning, the sense of his own
existence being likewise revealed to him thereby. Now, in the
sight of the 'One without a second', the whole of existence has no
being of its own: it is the expression of the one reality, that is to
say the totality of its aspects, manifestable and manifested, in the
midst of its very infinity. Things are no more than symbolic 'veils'
of their divine essence or, in a more immediate sense, of its ontological aspects; these aspects are the eternal archetypes of all that
is created.

If one understands creation in this way, it is revealed as a
multitude of more or less perfect images of God or of his qualities,
as a hierarchy of more or less pure truths leading towards the only
truth; for if God is the first origin and highest prototype of creation,
he is also its final end as Proverbs (16:4) testifies: 'YHVH has made
everything for his own purpose'.

The only reality cannot do otherwise than work for itself and
in itself. But in its pure selfness, it does not act or wish for any; in
it nothing whatsoever is determined, there is no distinction between subject and object, cause and effect, a god and a creation.
In this non-duality, God rests in himself, nameless, and without
any knowable aspect; it is only on this side of the supreme and
superintelligible essence that his knowledge 'makes its appearance',
which is to say his intelligent and intelligible being, including his
causal and efficient will. His being, his knowledge, his will and
his action are indivisible aspects of his ontological unity; this
unity is not affected by any of his attributes nor by any of his

61

manifestations: the One is what he is, knows himself, through himself, and works in himself for himself without becoming other than himself.

His work is the manifestation of all the aspects of his being in the midst of his being itself. In Sefirothic language it is said that *kether*, the supreme principle, sees itself through *hokhmah*, the 'wisdom' or first irradiation, in the mirror of *binah*, the 'intelligence' or infinite receptivity. In this supreme mirror God contemplates his seven lordly aspects: *hesed*, his 'grace'; *din*, his 'judgement'; *tifereth*, his 'beauty'; *netsah*, his 'victory'; *hod*, his 'glory'; *yesod*, the cosmic 'foundation' or his eternal act; and *malkhuth*, his 'kingdom', or immanence. The irradiations of his aspects come together in the last *Sefirah*, *malkhuth*, as in a lower mirror, and there form the multiple picture of what in reality is only one; this image of the infinite and indivisible aspects of the One is the Creation.

All created things emanate from God's being and from his knowledge; they are essentially his ontological and intelligible possibilities, the 'sparks' of his light, the 'ideas' that spring from his 'wisdom' or 'thought' like so many spiritual and existential 'rays'. 'When God designed to create the universe, his thought compassed all worlds at once, and by means of this thought were they all created, as it says, "In wisdom hast thou made them all" (Psalms 104:24). By this thought (*mahshabah*) – which is his wisdom (*hokhmah*) – were this world and the world above created. . . . All were created in one moment (the eternal moment of divine action). And he made this (terrestrial) world corresponding to the world above (the celestial and spiritual worlds which are themselves "pictures" of the infinite world of the *Sefiroth* or supreme archetypes), and everything which is above has its counterpart here below . . . and yet all constitute a unity (because of the causal sequence of all things and their essential identity with the only reality)' (*Zohar, Shemoth* 20a).

The knowledge of God is the *alpha* and *omega* of the work of creation. The world is born from the knowledge that God has of himself; and by the knowledge that the world has of God, it is reabsorbed into him. God made everything for this knowledge that unites to him; all other knowledge is only an ephemeral reflection of it. When the world sees God – through man – it sees its supreme archetype, its own uncreated fullness, and is effaced in its essence, in the infinite. This cognitive and deifying act is the ultimate fulfilment of the creative work; it is for that – for himself – that God created the world.

The knowledge of God does not depend on any science, but all human knowledge depends on it and derives from it. Receptivity alone, face to face with God, is enough, in principle, to obtain the influx of his light in which the spirit can see him. A science, even a revealed science such as cosmology, is only a possible, not an obligatory way of searching for knowledge of God; it is a way which makes it possible to receive the truth through his symbolic 'veils', that is through the worlds, on whatever scale. To see the eternal cause in cosmic effects raises a man above the illusions of the phenomenal world and brings him closer to reality. Baal-Shem[1] said: 'At times, man has to learn that there are an indefinite number of firmaments and spheres beyond, and that he himself is located in an insignificant spot on this small earth. But the entire universe is as nothing in the face of God, the Infinite, who brought about the "contraction" and made "room" in himself so that the worlds could be created in it. But although man may understand this with his mind, he is not able to ascend toward the higher worlds; and this is what is meant by: "The Lord appeared to me from afar" – he contemplates God from afar. But if he serves God with all his strength, he actualizes a great power in himself and rises in spirit, and suddenly pierces all the firmaments, and ascends beyond the angels, beyond the celestial "wheels", beyond the Serafim and the "thrones": and that is the perfect "service".'

[1] Israel ben Eliezer, called Baal-Shem (Master of the Divine Name), 1700–60, was the greatest Jewish saint of the last centuries. He founded Polish and Ukrainian Hasidism; this term comes from the word *hasid*, the 'devout' in regard to God. His movement developed towards the middle of the eighteenth century in Poland and spread into all the Slav countries; in the last century it included nearly four million adepts.

When Baal-Shem says that 'God, the infinite, brings about a "contraction" and makes "room" in himself where the worlds can be created', he is alluding to the Kabbalistic doctrine of *tsimtsum*. The term *tsimtsum* can be translated by 'contraction', 'restriction', 'retreat', or 'concentration'; it had been used in Jewish esotericism chiefly since Isaac Luria (1534-72) to describe the divine mystery on which creation depends. 'The Holy One, blessed by he, withdrew his powerful light from one part of himself, and left a void to serve as "a place" for cosmic expansion'; it concerns 'that part of the divine essence in which the light was weakened to allow the existence of souls, angels and the material worlds.'

Through this symbolic language, the Kabbalah then tries to express the mysterious genesis of the finite in the midst of the infinite. In reality, God, the absolute One, has no 'parts', but an infinity of possibilities, of which only the creatural possibilities have the illusory appearance of separate forms; in themselves, these forms are integrated, as eternal archetypes, in the all-possibility of the One. As for that 'part from which the light has been withdrawn' to make room for the 'place' of the cosmos, it is nothing other than the receptivity of God that actualizes itself in the midst of his unlimited fullness; this receptivity has a transcendent aspect and an immanent aspect: 'above', it is identified with *binah*, the 'supreme mother', which is eternally filled with the infinite and luminous emanation of the 'father', *hokhmah*; 'below', it is *malkhuth*, the 'lower mother', or cosmic receptivity of God. The latter absorbs both the influx from the *Sefiroth* of mercy which are luminous and overflowing, and the influx from the *Sefiroth* of rigour which are 'dark' or 'empty'; that is why, in contrast to *binah*, which is always revealed as filled with the infinite, *malkhuth*, or divine immanence, can take on the appearance of a dark void in the midst of its radiant fullness. Indeed, *binah* is said to be 'without all rigour, although rigour emanates from it'; while *malkhuth* receives the emanations of rigour together with those of grace, to produce and dominate the cosmos and hold it in equilibrium through the interpenetration of the two simultaneously opposite and complementary influxes.

Now, the rigour which emanates from *binah* is *din*, 'judgement' or universal discernment, the principle of concentration, distinction and limitation; it produces *tsimtsum*, divine 'contraction', in the heart of *malkhuth*, the plastic cause. Through the effect of *tsimtsum*, the divine fullness withdraws to a certain extent from the 'lower mother', and awakens creative receptivity in her; the latter, when actualized, takes on the aspect of the void or 'place of the world', ready to receive cosmic manifestation. Then, all created possibilities spring up from the existential seed which is left behind by divine fullness on its withdrawal – as a luminous 'residue' (*reshimu*) in the midst of immanent emptiness. Thus, thanks to the divine 'contraction' and to the void it brings about in the *shekhinah*, the expansion of the world takes place; and everything living in the immanence of God is a small world created in the image of the macrocosm: it is a void to which life is given by a luminous 'residue' of the only reality, by a central and divine 'spark' that projects onto it the reflection of some eternal archetype.

The Kabbalah expresses the same cosmogonical process in other symbolic terms as the *pargod* or cosmic 'curtain'. The *Idra Rabba Kadisha* (the 'great and holy assembly', included in the *Zohar*) says of the 'Ancient of Ancients' that 'he draws a curtain down before him' through which his kingdom begins to take shape. This image and that of the *tsimtsum* not only point to the same truth but from one point of view also complement each other. Thus it can be said that God appears to 'withdraw' himself into himself to the extent that he draws down a 'curtain' before him. The 'curtain' hangs before him like a darkness; and this darkness in reality is nothing other than his cosmic receptivity, which allows his reality to appear through it as a light. But his infinite light appears through the dark veil only in a 'weakened', fragmented and limited way, which is the mode of existence of the finite.

God is hidden in everything he creates, somewhat in the way that light is contained in the innumerable reflections that produce a mirage. To go further in this symbolism, it could be said that the desert where the mirage is produced represents the 'void' or the 'place' of the world made by *tsimtsum*, and the imperceptible screen on which appear the vanishing forms that lead the pilgrim astray represents the '*pargod*', which is the 'curtain' or 'mirror' of the *shekhinah*. In fact, in the face of the 'One without a second', creation – the apparition of a 'second' – as well as the creative causes themselves, come to appear as existential illusions. That is why the Kabbalah brings in a third idea, in addition to those of *tsimtsum* and *pargod*, to define the nature of creation, namely, *habel*, 'vanity', derived from Ecclesiastes (1:2): 'Vanity of vanities (*habel habalim*), all is vanity!' The *Zohar* (*Shemoth* 10b) teaches on this subject: 'King Solomon, in his book (Ecclesiastes), treated of seven "vanities" (*habalim*, lit. breaths) upon which the world stands, namely, the seven (Sefirothic) pillars (of universal construction) which sustain the world in (causal) correspondence with (their first created effects) the seven firmaments, which are called respectively *Vilon, Rakiya, Shehakim, Zebul, Ma'on, Makhon, Araboth*. It was concerning them that Solomon said: "Vanity of vanities . . . all is vanity" (*ibid*, 1:1). As there are seven firmaments, with others (existential planes such as the seven earths and seven hells) cleaving to them and issuing from them, so there are seven *habalim* and others emanating from these (and filling all creation), and Solomon in his wisdom referred to them all (as well as to their causes and archetypes, the seven *Sefiroth* of construction).'

The Kabbalah does not say that the seven cosmological *Sefiroth* are illusions in themselves, for they represent the creative aspects of one and the same reality; nevertheless, in so far as they project the mirage of an existential multitude in the midst of its undifferentiated unity, they manifest as so many principles of illusion or causal 'vanities'. But if they are considered outside of their relation with creation, they are integrated into absolute unity. In so far as the One is looking at himself alone, he does not go out of his supreme tri-unity, *kether–hokhmah–binah*; but when he wishes to contemplate the creative possibilities in himself, he opens his 'seven eyes' or 'Sefiroth of construction', projecting all the cosmic 'vanities' through their look. 'Vanity', according to Ecclesiastes, is to be found 'under the sun' – a symbol of the Sefirah tifereth, which synthesizes the six active Sefiroth of 'construction'—and is made upon the earth; now the 'earth' is one of the synonyms of malkhuth, the receptive and substantial Sefirah of cosmic 'construction': there alone, in the divine immanence, the mirage of creation is produced, maintained and effaced. 'That is why the beginning of Genesis – says the Tikkune Zohar – is concerned only with the elohim (principle of immanence) designating the shekhinah (and not with the transcendental principle, YHVH). Everything created, from the hayoth and the serafim (higher angels) down to the smallest worm on the earth, lives in elohim and through elohim . . . The creation is the work of the shekhinah who takes care of it as a mother cares for her children.'

The entire creation is an illusory projection of the transcendental aspects of God into the 'mirror' of his immanence. The Zohar notes, in fact, that the verb baro, 'to create', implies the idea of 'creating an illusion'. But although the creation is by nature illusory, it contains something of reality; for every reflection of reality, even remote, broken up and transient, necessarily possesses something of its cause. Even if the creation is taken as being pure illusion, that real something which constitutes its essence still cannot be excluded. Illusion itself is not a mere nothingness, for there cannot be any such thing. By its very existence it would no longer be nothing; illusion is a 'mixture' of the real and the ephemeral or – in Kabbalistic terminology – of 'light' and 'darkness'.

Creation is made from the 'dark void' that God established in the midst of his luminous fullness and which he then filled with his existential reflections. This 'dark void' is the 'mirror' or plane of cosmic reflection, inherent in the receptivity of the shekhinah. Indeed, receptivity is both emptiness and darkness; but while the nature of the void is transparency or translucence, that of darkness is opacity or contraction. Thus, when the creative influx of the Sefiroth fills the receptivity of the 'lower mother', its emptiness or translucence transmits the divine radiation in all the directions of the cosmos, while its darkness contracts, condenses and becomes substance enveloping light. In its first and celestial condensation, substance is still subtle and resplendent with the radiation that only lightly veils it; but it becomes opaque and gross in its corporeal and terrestrial solidification, which hides the light from above, as thick clouds mask the sun.

The 'vanity' of things consists in this darkness which fleetingly takes on the appearance of substance; however, substance becomes a mirror of truth when the forms it assumes are recognized as the symbolic expressions of the eternal archetypes, which are none other than the divine aspects.

3

The ten fundamental aspects of God, or *Sefiroth*, are manifested at first on the macrocosmic level in the form of ten heavens. The three supreme *Sefiroth*, *kether–hokhmah–binah*, are revealed in the three 'heavens of heavens', the triple immanent principle: that is, *shekhinah–metatron–avir*. *Shekhinah* is the immanence of *kether*, the presence of divine reality in the midst of the cosmos. *Metatron*, the manifestation of *hokhmah* and the active aspect of the *shekhinah*, is the principial form from which all created forms emanate; *avir*, the ether, is a manifestation of *binah*:[1] it is the passive aspect of *shekhinah*, its cosmic receptivity, which gives birth to every created substance, whether subtle or corporeal. The triple immanent principle, *shekhinah–metatron–avir*, in its undifferentiated unity, constitutes the spiritual and prototypical 'world of creation': *olam haberiyah*.

The seven *Sefiroth* of universal construction, *hesed–din–tifereth–netsah–hod–yesod–malkhuth*, which emanate from the supreme triunity, are the causes and archetypes of the seven created heavens; the latter issue from the three 'heavens of heavens', as the con-

[1] Sometimes *avir* is identified, by metaphysical transposition, with the supreme principle, *kether*; it is the substantial indistinction of the ether which, in this case, serves as a 'symbol' of the indeterminateness of the absolute essence.

stituent degrees of the 'world of formation', *olam hayetsirah*. In this world all creatures undergo their first and subtle formation; it is situated beyond space and time, in the indefinite expansion and duration of the supra-terrestrial cosmos. *Olam hayetsirah* is imperceptible to the senses and serves as a dwelling place for souls – before or after they pass through the earth – for angels and for spirits.

Between the seven subtle heavens and the 'seven earths' which issue from them, are situated as further manifestations of the *Sefiroth* of construction, the seven degrees of the 'lower Eden' or earthly Paradise, inhabited by angels and blessed souls; in this intermediary world there exist also darkened inversions of the heavens, namely the seven hells or abodes of the demons and of the damned.

The corporeal universe comprising the 'seven earths', is called the 'world of fact', *olam ha'asiyah*; it is conditioned by time, space, the material elements and, from the microcosmic point of view, by sensory perception. The seven earths represent so many different states of our universe; they are described as 'seven countries', hierarchically 'super-posed and all populated'; one of them, the 'higher earth', is our own, which the six others resemble without attaining its perfection; in the same way their inhabitants possess only an incomplete or unbalanced kind of human form. On the other hand, the seven *Sefiroth* of construction – which are also called the 'seven days of (principial) creation' – are manifested in time in the following septenaries: the seven days of the week; the seven years forming a 'sabbatical' cycle; the seven times seven years between one 'Jubilee' and another; the seven thousand years representing a great cycle of existence; and the 'seven times seven thousand years' ending at the fiftieth millenium, on the 'great Jubilee', when the world is reintegrated into the divine principle.[1] Finally, the seven *Sefiroth* of construction determine

---

[1] When the Kabbalah says that the total duration of the world is fifty thousand years, this figure should be taken as a symbolic expression of the law which constitutes its eternal foundation. This law resides in the mystery of the seven *Sefiroth* of construction, each one of which recapitulates, in its way, the

the six directions of space and their spiritual centre, called the 'Holy of Holies'.

Man is the most perfect image of universal reality in the whole of creation; he is the 'incarnated' recapitulation of all the cosmic degrees and of their divine archetypes. Indeed, as we saw in the preceding chapter, through his spiritual faculties, psychic virtues and corporeal forms, he represents the most evident symbol of the ten *Sefiroth*, and his integral personality embraces all the worlds: his pure and uncreated being is identified with the Sefirothic 'world of emanation' (*olam ha'atsiluth*); his spirit, with the prototypical 'world of creation' (*olam haberiyah*); his soul with the subtle 'world of formation' (*olam hayetsirah*); and his body, with the sensory 'world of fact' (*olam ha'asiyah*). The law of man, the Decalogue, is a manifestation of the ten *Sefiroth*, as is the 'sacred community' of Israel, which is complete only when ten Jewish men come together.

The human being is the principal 'point of intersection' of the Sefirothic rays in the midst of the cosmos; through him, the divine riches are revealed in all their spiritual radiance and by the explicit symbolism of thought, word, forms and corporeal gestures. Of all beings, man alone – in his perfect state – is the one being whom God causes to participate fully in his infinite knowledge; and through man's intermediary God brings everything back to himself.

4

If creation is the image of God, cosmogony operates – just like a reflected projection – by the law of inversion or, more precisely, by inverse analogy. This law derives from the principle of divine 'contraction', *tsimtsum*; by the effect of this 'contraction', the infinite, *en sof*, appears as *nekuda*, the causal 'point' or supreme

---

whole. Thus one is faced with a unity of 'seven times seven' or forty-nine *Sefirothic* degrees, which are manifested through as many cyclical phases, its total duration being that of the indefinite existence of the cosmos; these forty-nine degrees issue from *binah* and return to it. *Binah*, as their 'end', is the 'fiftieth' degree, or the supreme and prototypical 'Jubilee'.

'centre' of the finite, and the limits of the finite are extended and take on the appearance of unlimited existence. The 'contraction' or first inversion is reflected in the midst of existence itself, with the actualization of a multitude of 'central points', each surrounded by an expanse, which serves both as 'veil' and 'mirror' for its contents. All these 'centres' are connected among themselves and with the 'supreme Centre', by the 'middle pillar' or universal axis, which is none other than the creative, regulating and redemptive 'ray' of the divine principle. The 'spheres of activity', which surround their respective centres, are all the worlds, great and small, together making up the cosmic expanse; whether they appear as worlds properly so called, as beings or as things, each of these spheres constitutes, therefore, the 'envelope' or 'shell' of such and such a 'kernel' or existential point of departure, hier-archically included in the 'middle pillar'. Finally, as was explained in the last chapter, every 'point' representing the centre, the immediate principle or prototype of such a world, itself functions as the 'field of action' of a higher centre, and so on up to the supreme centre, which is its own 'sphere of activity' embracing all the others.

Thus we are confronted by an indefinite series of existential states, formed by as many 'inversions' or exteriorizations of their respective points of departure. We have just seen that all these 'points' are co-ordinated, in accordance with the law of causality, in the universal axis, which is the 'descent' of the 'supreme point' across the centre or 'heart' of everything; thus, each thing, in spite of its dependence on what is hierarchically above it, contains in its innermost depth the 'centre of centres', the real presence of God. Every created thing is in its own way a synthesis of the whole of creation, whether in a conscious, developed or seminal mode and it includes in its essence the principle itself. The principle or universal and divine centre is not comparable, therefore, to a point or geometric axis, localized in any one place:[1] it is the omnipresent medium.

[1] It should be made clear that if the divine immanent centre is not 'local-ized' in any one place – because it penetrates all – it nevertheless reveals itself

Terrestrial man, 'last born' of the creation, is the 'lower point' where cosmogony stops in its creative inversions and returns toward the 'supreme point'. When this 'inversion of inversions' starts to work in man, it is said that he is seized by *teshubah*, 'conversion', 'repentance', or the 'return' to God; indeed, when man 'performs *teshubah*', with all his heart, all his soul, and all his might, he ends by being absorbed into his pure and divine 'self' and by integrating – within himself – the whole of existence in the cause. This is given to man by the mystery of his inner and universal person which embraces everything from the terrestrial 'world of fact' to the very principle of the 'world of emanation'; that is why the voluntary 'return' of man to God involves the 'return' of all the worlds. 'Great is *teshubah*, for it heals the world. Great is *teshubah*, for it reaches the throne of glory. Great is *teshubah*, for it brings about redemption' (Talmud, *Yoma* 86 a).

By his absorption in God, man actualizes universal deliverance in himself and thereby 'hastens' cosmic redemption. The latter occurs when the entire multitude of subtle and corporeal manifestations has been exhausted in the midst of the two created worlds. At that moment the 'grand Jubilee' takes place, the total and final deliverance;[1] it is the ultimate phase of *tsimtsum*, the 'inversion of inversions', which is not only the 'contraction' of the corporeal universe, but of the entire cosmic expanse: the 'withdrawal' of the whole creation into its uncreated centre and

---

by preference in a sanctified place or being; the latter thereby represents the living expression of the universal centre.

[1] The definitive reintegration of the cosmos into the principle, which is to be accomplished at the end of 'seven times seven millenia' or great cycles of existence, is prefigured by transitory restorations of the paradisal state, which take place every 'seventh millenium' or 'great Sabbath' of creation. As we shall explain in the chapter on the corporeal world, one of these 'moments of rest' or transient absorptions of the created into the divine immanence was the cycle of the *Fiat Lux*, the other, that of the adamic *Eden*; according to tradition, we are now at the dawn of a new cosmic Sabbath, the 'Reign of the Messiah'.

principle. Then, every immanent spiritual light regains its transcendent brightness, and every terrestrial and celestial substance is reabsorbed in the 'higher ether' (*avira ilaah*), which is eternally integrated into the infinite essence. Such is the return of the cosmic 'image' to divine reality.

IV The Kingdom of Heaven

Who coverest thyself with light as with a garment,
Who stretcheth out the heavens like a curtain.

Psalms 104:2

I

Study of the heavens in Jewish esotericism is based on the doctrine of the *Sefiroth*, which are the causes and archetypes of the celestial worlds. Some notion of these worlds can be formed thanks to the real correspondences between the Sefirothic 'models' and their symbols and by reading traditional descriptions of the heavens; but it will be no more than a dim, mental reflection of true knowledge of the heavenly kingdom. The Kabbalah declares that such knowledge can only be obtained through the 'heart's seeing', the perception of the universal spirit which dwells in the innermost depths of man. 'Here is a mystery of mysteries, which none but the adepts in esoteric wisdom can fathom – one of those mysteries of the Holy Lamp (cognomen of Rabbi Simeon bar Yohai), who could expound the mystery of every firmament and of every being who officiates in each of them' (*Zohar, Terumah* 164b).

Here is what the Kabbalah reveals concerning the mystery of the genesis of the heavens: 'When the Holy One was about to create the world he robed himself in the primordial light and created the heavens. At first the light was at the right (the active and spiritual side) and the darkness at the left (the receptive and substantial side). What, then, did the Holy One do? He merged the one into the other and from them formed the heavens: *shamaim* (heavens) is composed of *esh* and *maim* (fire [spiritual light] and water [subtle substance] i.e. right and left). He brought them together and harmonized them, and when they were united as one, he stretched them out like a curtain . . .' (*ibid.*).

In other terms, *kether* wraps itself in its first causal emanation, *hokhmah*, and surrounds *hokhmah* with its receptivity, *binah*; and the radiation of the active principle completely fills the receptivity of the passive cause.[1] Their common emanation is the uncreated unity of the seven '*Sefiroth* of (cosmic) construction' which are the eternal foundation of the seven created heavens. But before these heavens are brought forth, the first and transcendental causes are made manifest in their triple immanence: *Shekhinah–metatron–avir*, the immediate principles of creation, which are called the 'heaven of heavens'. The *shekhinah*, or real presence of *kether*, wraps itself in *metatron*, its active and spiritual manifestation – which is the immanence of *hokhmah* – and in *avir*, its cosmic and substantial receptivity, the ether, which is the emanation of *binah*. The *shekhinah* then unites the spiritual radiation of *metatron* with the subtle manifestation of *avir*, and by this forms the heavens.

'Seven heavens are stretched out and stored in the supernal treasure-house (the "world of [subtle] formation") . . . and over them is one firmament (the prototypical "world of creation", or world of the three "heavens of heavens") which has no colour (no distinct aspect) and no place in the world of cognition (i.e. discursive and rational knowledge), and is outside the range of contemplation (of created beings); but, though hidden, it diffuses light to all and speeds them each on its fitting orbit . . .' (*ibid.* 164b).

'The ten curtains of the Tabernacle symbolized the ten firmaments (and the latter, the ten *Sefiroth*), and their mystery can be comprehended only by the wise of heart (in which the triple celestial principle, *shekhinah–metatron–avir*, dwells and is revealed); he who grasps this (spiritually, or suprarationally) attains great wisdom and penetrates into the mysteries of the universe . . .' (*ibid.*).

---

[1] Let it be made clear that all this is concerned with one unique principal action; *hokhmah* and *binah* emanate simultaneously from *kether*, the dark receptivity of the 'mother' being entirely filled with the luminous fullness of the 'father'; these two complementary principles are never in any way separate. They are not, therefore, really two; the created being, man, sees them as differentiated, being himself subject to distinction. In reality, *hokhmah* and *binah* are indivisible and inseparable aspects of *kether*, the One.

2

According to the Kabbalistic treatises on the *hekhaloth*, or celestial 'palaces' – from which we shall quote, as well as from the Talmudic texts dealing with the 'world above' – the seven created heavens represent a like number of dwelling places in hierarchical order one above the other, for human souls before or after their stay upon earth, as well as for the angels and spirits. In the centre of each 'palace' resides 'celestial man' in the form of a particular prophetic manifestation; in other words, the spirit of a prophet presides over each of the heavens, revealing the divine in the light of the *Sefirah* of which he is the 'messenger' and which rules over that particular heaven. This prophetic spirit is surrounded by all the human souls which 'belong' to it, that is to say which are ascending towards God or descending from him by the way of a particular Sefirothic manifestation; and the prophet is assisted, in his mediatory function, by the angels and spirits in movement in his 'palace' and acting under the influence of the divine aspect which characterizes it. Human souls surround the divine centre of each heaven and the angels and spirits surround the dwelling place of the souls. The nearness of these human beings to the divinity renders their heavenly existence purely contemplative and unitive, whereas the angels and spirits represent chiefly celestial powers and functions, as 'servants' or 'messengers'.

'There are seven heavens above and another seven below corresponding to them': these are the seven 'palaces' of the 'upper Eden', or heavenly Paradise, to which correspond those of the 'lower Eden', or earthly Paradise. A soul dwelling in a particular 'palace' of the lower Eden contemplates the same divine aspect as a soul dwelling in the corresponding 'palace' in the upper Eden, with the difference, however, that it sees the Sefirothic manifestation through a wrapping, a 'veil' which no longer exists for the soul 'above' and which enjoys a more direct vision of the divine immanence. But whatever made such a soul worthy to dwell in the lower Paradise also leads it to a corresponding dwelling in the celestial Paradise when it has remained in the lower Eden 'as long as was necessary to make it ready to ascend to the upper Eden'.

Thus the lower 'palaces' are viewed as the anterooms of the upper 'palaces' and the hierarchy of souls 'below' corresponds with that of the souls 'above'.

The celestial hierarchy, as has been shown, is founded in the last analysis on the eternal 'relationships' between the Sefirothic archetypes; but in spite of this the order 'above' cannot, in many respects, be grasped by the separative reason of man. The heavens are the orderly steps of the 'ladder' which is 'set upon the earth, its top reaching to the (supreme) heaven', above which 'stands YHVH'; yet, 'since all beings experience (in their deepest part) an irresistible need to come nearer to the "supreme point", like one starved and burning with the desire for food, the (Sefirothic) rays shooting out from the "supreme point", form at their lower extremity another "point": this is the "point below", *elohim* (divine immanence); and it is nevertheless the same light as above, the infinite (YHVH; for – say the Scriptures – YHVH is *elohim*).' Thus the heavenly 'ladder' is like a circle the end of which meets the beginning, so that the souls of the righteous find the One 'below' just as they find him 'on high'; and this is not the only point of view from which the superiority of one heaven in respect to the others is seen to be relative: it is also relative because each heaven represents the manifestation of one particular perfection or 'unique' quality of God, which in its own way embraces the other divine aspects. Lastly, the celestial hierarchy can also, in geometrical symbolism, be thought of in a horizontal form: it is said that the seventh heaven encloses the six others in its indefinite expanse which is the 'surface of the waters'; this surface reflects all cosmic possibilities. From this point of view, the seven *hekhaloth* or 'palaces' are situated on one and the same plane, namely the celestial realm, inasmuch as they are 'successive entrances' – hierarchically disposed – leading to their common end: the throne of glory.

Besides the hierarchy of prophetic spirits and other spiritual and angelic powers often becomes lost in the 'middle pillar', where it is integrated into the indistinct omnipresence of the One. The order of this hierarchy is complicated by the descent or ascent of a certain prophet or angel, from his chief dwelling place to a celestial 'region' where he appears in the light of a divine manifestation other than that which is characteristically his. As for the angels, the Kabbalah makes it clear that 'each one has a well-defined field of action, so that no one of them may trespass on the domain of another, not so much as by a hair's breadth, unless expressly authorized to do so'; but at the same time it states that they 'ascend and descend' in the immense kingdom of the heavens: on the 'lower regions' as well as in the 'higher', 'flashes' of the primordial and order-making lightning of the *hayoth* appear, the 'massed knowledge' or illumination of the *kerubim*, the purifying and sanctifying 'fires' of the *serafim*, the spiritual and spherical 'vibrations' of the *ofanim*, as well as the 'colours', the 'sounds' or 'voices' of the Archangels, who are above all others the celestial mediators between God and humanity. It should be added that the angels, who are spiritual 'fires' in the presence of God, are transformed into etheric 'winds' when they have a mission to accomplish on earth, where created beings would not be able to bear them in their true aspect.[1] Furthermore, stress is laid in the tradition on the fact that all the angelic powers and their multiple manifestations are linked together in a variety of ways and in as many aspects of the one creative, revelatory and redemptive act of God.

3

The *shekhinah* or divine immanence externalizes, by its radiation, *metatron*, all its cosmic possibilities, which are both spiritual 'sparks' and existential 'seeds'; it then clothes them in their created and celestial 'habit', by the first subtle and differentiated manifestation of *avir*. This first expansion of the subtle 'waters' issuing from the undifferentiated ether constitutes the indefinite 'surface' of the existential 'ocean': the seventh heaven, the manifestation of the *Sefirah hesed*, 'grace'. Whereas the 'heaven of

---

[1] Cf. Psalm 104:4: '. . . who makest winds thy messengers, the flaming fire thy ministers', and the Haggadic commentary on this in *Yalkut hadash* (115a).

heavens', which overhangs this first cosmic expanse like an immense sun, never emerges from its principial immutability, the 'surface of the (created) waters' is moved by the 'wind of *Elohim*', the creative and redemptive act of the triple celestial principle; each one of these 'waves' – souls, spirits or angels – is a subtle vibration, inhabited and illuminated by a spiritual 'spark'. This first 'mixture' of spirit and substance has given the seventh heaven the name *Araboth*,[1] a term which is often translated as 'clouds', 'plains' or 'desert', but which is derived from the root *ARB* indicating something mixed; we have seen that the same idea is to be found at the base of the word *shamaïm*, 'heavens', which is a composite of *esh* (spiritual 'fire') and of *maïm* (substantial 'waters'). 'It is the seventh firmament and it is called *araboth* (mixtures), because it is composed of fire and water . . .' (*Zohar*, *Terumah* 165a).

When the spiritual vibration of the divine light falls on the subtle expanse of *Araboth*, it produces therein the primordial, creative and redemptive sound or 'cry'. Each creature which appears on the 'surface of the waters', whether issuing from God or returning from the depths of the cosmic 'ocean', 'bursts' into one 'cry of joy' and expands indefinitely like a 'wave' of light and of sound: it spreads out over the whole plane of the sea of existence, the whole expanse of *Araboth*, illuminated by the divine sun. Every 'wave' becomes the whole cosmic 'ocean', the whole 'mirror' of the living God; and while its substance becomes one with that of all the other 'waves', its spirit, the divine 'spark', becomes infinite light. The 'cry of joy' accompanying this total union is the first and inarticulate invocation of the universal name of God: the utterance of the primordial sound, brought about by the Creator in action as well as by all the beings who enter the seventh heaven. 'The Holy One, blessed be he, loves this firmament more than any of the other firmaments and delights in perfecting it with supernal beauty. Therefore does it say (Psalms 68:5):

[1] The name *Araboth*, as well as the names of the six other created heavens which we are going to mention – according to Talmud, *Hagigah* 12 – are derived from the Scriptures.

"Extol him that rideth upon *Araboth* . . . and rejoice before him"
. . . he who comes before that firmament must do so in joy, and
not in sadness, for there all is pure joy with no trace of sadness or
gloom' (*Zohar, Terumah* 165a).

After having known the unitive and beatific state of *Araboth*,
created beings have to descend into 'darkened' existence there to
fulfil their destiny, their cosmic 'function'; on coming back from
their 'pilgrimage' and arriving again in the seventh heaven, they
are passively reabsorbed in God, with the exception of the
righteous ones, who there contemplate the supreme mysteries and
are united with him in an active and definitive way; as for the
created beings who are united with God only in a passive manner,
they may be reprojected into the cosmos. Let us make it clear that
all human souls – unlike other created beings, whose relation with
God is passive – are destined to be actively united with him; this is
why, on returning from their cosmic 'journey' insufficiently prepared for their deification, they are sent back, either to one of the
six heavens below *Araboth*, in order to come towards the divine
through a Sefirothic manifestation, or else into a cycle of 'transmigration' (*gilgul*), in order to repair the faults they have committed in their former life; or again they may be condemned
to purification in hell, which, however, in the Jewish tradition,
does not imply 'eternal damnation', since hell also will finally
be reintegrated in *Araboth* together with all the other cosmic
degrees.

Araboth is in fact the heaven from which all created beings
come out from God and re-enter into him and in which they all
appear in their pristine and purely luminous form, at the same
time as the original manifestations of the cosmic principles. This
is why the Talmud (*Hagigah* 12b) says: 'In *Araboth* are justice
(from which flows equilibrium in the creation), judgement (or the
first discernment of spirits), charity (which unites everything with
God), the realms of life, of peace and of blessing; there are to be
found the souls of the just, the spirits and souls waiting to be
created (that is to say who spring forth from the divine radiation
in order to become clothed in subtle substance), and the (spiritual)

dew by means of which, in the future, the Holy One, blessed be he, will resurrect the dead. There dwell the *ofanim*, the *serafim*, the holy *hayoth*, the ministering angels, the throne of glory and the king, the living God, sublime and exalted, who stands above them in the cloud, as it is said (Psalms 68:5): "Extol him that rideth upon the clouds (*Araboth*); *Yah* is his name."'

4

Araboth, the seventh heaven or 'seventh degree of the (divine) throne', is ruled by the Messiah, as the *Idra Rabba Kadisha* testifies: 'The Messiah king was destined to sit on the seventh (degree of heaven or "throne"). There are six of them (celestial or spiritual degrees) and the spirit of the ancient of days (the principle of all cycles or states of existence), which stands above them, is the seventh (this is the spirit of *Yah* "who rides on *Araboth*") . . . and in the days of the Messiah king "They shall teach no more every man his neighbour" (Jeremiah 31:34), since this spirit, which embraces all spirits, will make known to each one the wisdom and intelligence, the counsel and might, the knowledge and the fear of YHVH (cf. Isaiah 11:2); for this is the spirit that embraces all spirits.'

The spirit of the Messiah is that of the Ancient of Days or of *Yah*, his real presence in the seventh heaven: this is the 'spirit of *Elohim*' or of the divine immanence, which 'hovers over the face of the waters' and illuminates them. The form of the Messiah is that of 'celestial man', *metatron*, 'seated upon the throne'; and his substance is the pure emanation of *avir*, the ether. Thus the Messiah is one with the triple immanent principle, *shekhinah-metatron-avir*; he is the universal mediator who, from the seventh heaven, enters the 'heaven of heavens' – or the celestial 'holy of holies' – and reemerges from it to manifest the divine will to all the created worlds. He it is who performs, in *Araboth*, the redemptive act in the name of the 'living God' and who will perform the same on earth at the end of time. The mystery of his perfection lies, in fact, not only in the predominance of his uncreated nature, but also in that his created nature is purely redemptive; the

Messiah precedes, rules and saves the whole of creation. 'When the creation of the (universal) world began, the Messiah king (already) was, for he came to the spirit (of God) even before the world was created' (*Pesikta Rab.* 152b). He descends and ascends through all the heavens in order to perform, with the prophets there abiding, the universal saving function. This heavenly ministry is reflected on the temporal and terrestrial plane in the succession of prophets who, all of them, bring the Messianic light, but each in a particular form, according to the Sefirothic manifestation predominating in that particular phase or part of humanity. It is only at the end of time that the Messiah will himself descend to earth, there to pour out the whole of his grace and enlighten the whole world; he is to descend in the form of two different manifestations: the first time as the 'son of Joseph' who has to die, and a second time as the 'son of David', conqueror of God's enemies and saviour of the 'rest of his sheep'.[1]

Among the souls of the righteous surrounding the Messiah in *Araboth* are those of the prophets; even when the prophets' souls are carrying out their spiritual ministry in one of the lower heavens, they are connected with the seventh heaven by the constant 'union of all the celestial palaces'. This union takes place in the 'middle pillar', where the prophets dwell, whatever their celestial sphere of activity; by that very fact they are directly connected with the divine principle 'who rides on *Araboth*'. The souls of the prophets, like those of all human beings which, in their original purity, surround the Messiah are higher than the spirits and angels; they proceed directly from *shekhinah* and are identified essentially with the unity of all the *Sefiroth*, 'principal

[1] A striking analogy will be noticed with the Christian doctrine of the 'suffering' or 'crucified Christ' and the 'victorious' or 'glorious Christ', with the history of Jesus, son of Joseph, and the apocalyptic vision of the 'son of David' (Revelation 22:16). As in Christianity, Jesus of Nazareth is identified in Islam also with the Messiah (*Al-Masîh*); all orthodox religions, furthermore, expect the advent of a saviour at the end of time, whatever may be the name given to 'him who is to come'.

man' (*adam kadmon*). This does not apply to the angels and spirits, which, although they issue from *metatron*, yet have as their respective archetype only one or another *Sefirah*, that is, a particular aspect of 'man above', or of divine being, and not the unity of all his attributes; from this it results that 'below' they express only some particular quality of *adam kadmon* – or of *metatron*, which is his immanence – whereas the human soul in its perfection expresses him totally.

The spirits are particularizations of the radiation of *metatron*; their 'colourless' supraformal light is broken, on entering creation, into myriads of rays and sparks; all these spiritual lights take on the 'colour', according to the quality of their respective 'function', of some Sefirothic 'shade', and radiate with greater or lesser intensity but without assuming any other particular formal appearance. On the contrary, 'the angels are spirits' which, according to their mission, are clothed in one or another celestial 'apparel'; while the spirits properly so-called retain their relatively 'informal' aspect, the angels are clothed in the most diverse appearances, varying according to the nature of their 'mandate', and dependent on a specific mixture of subtle elements and of a corresponding form.

5

In *Araboth*, the human souls expand in the light of him who is seated on the 'throne of glory', while the angels and spirits serve 'at the feet of the throne'; now, the 'feet of the throne' are none other than the four universal peripheral 'axes' issuing by refraction from the 'middle pillar'; they are the four *hayoth* or 'living beings' of Ezekiel's vision, the supreme spirits or angels. They 'carry the throne' and their 'sweat' produces the 'river of fire' (*nahar dinur*), or subtle substance in its igneous and 'terrible' aspect. All the other spirits and angels are grouped below the *hayoth*, by which the 'four (supreme) cardinal points' are fixed, that is to say the supraspacial confines of the cosmic expanse, from which proceed the cardinal points of space; the four subtle elements and the four corporeal elements also flow out from the *hayoth*, as well as all the other quaternaries by which existence is conditioned.

The 'throne', in its fullness, is the first and spiritual crystallization of all creatural possibilities before they are set in motion in
the midst of the cosmos. When the 'throne' assumes its dynamic
aspect and cosmic manifestation begins to move, it is called the
divine 'chariot' (*merkabah*); then the four *hayoth*, or peripheral
axes of creation, spring from the 'throne' become 'chariot', like
'lightning darting in all directions', measuring all the dimensions
and all the planes of manifested existence. Under the aspect of
'torches', 'brilliant lights' or spiritual 'flashes' of lightning, the
hayoth are also called *kerubim*, 'those who are close' to the living
God, that is to say who emanate directly from God in action.
While the hayothic axes are travelling in all the directions of
the cosmos, out of them come 'wheels' (*ofanim*), or angelic
powers, which play a part in actualizing the spherical forms and
cyclical movements of the created; their spiral vibrations – as it
were 'a wheel within another wheel' – are called 'whirlwinds'
(*galgalim*).

Aside from these angelological teachings, which go back to the
vision of Ezekiel, the prophecy of Isaiah needs to be mentioned,
according to which the divine throne is surrounded by the *serafim*,
'the burning ones'. The seraphim are so named because they con-
sume or purify everything they touch with their spiritual fire; by
means of their six wings or celestial powers – manifesting the six
active '*Sefiroth* of (cosmic) construction' – they co-operate in the
development of the six cosmogonic phases which evolve from
their point of departure in *Araboth*, the 'holy of holies' or celestial
'Sabbath', in the form of the six heavens, the six directions of space
and the 'six days' or great phases of time.

The revelation of Isaiah (6:1–3) is as follows: '. . . I saw the
Lord (immanent, *Adonai*, synonym of the *shekhinah*, revealed
under the aspect of "celestial man", *metatron*) sitting upon a throne
high and lifted up (above creation) and his train (the first emanations of uncreated substance, *avir*) filled the Temple (synonym of
the seventh heaven). Above him stood the *serafim* (as so many of
his spiritual manifestations): each one had six wings; with twain
he covered his face, and with twain he covered his feet, and with

twain he did fly. And one called unto another (manifesting the inarticulate "voice" of God) and said (in revelatory articulation or utterance of the divine "Word"): Holy, holy, holy is the Y H V H of Hosts (God of cosmic powers). The whole earth (the whole of creation) is full of his glory (or omnipresence)!'

According to the Kabbalah, Isaiah saw the same reality as Ezekiel, but revealed the world of the throne, or angelic world, in a far more summary form than the latter, who, by cyclical necessity, brought an analysis of it. Where Ezekiel describes the angels in various forms having human and animal aspects, or again as 'coals of fire' and 'wheels of chrysolite' (forms symbolizing the various modes of God's celestial activity), Isaiah on the other hand seems only to have seen the 'wings' of the seraphim, with which they covered their faces and their feet while hovering before the divine throne; this symbolism can be taken to show that the angels possessed no form properly so-called but were distinguished one from the other by 'faculties', 'tendencies' or principial 'attitudes'. From Isaiah's description and the meaning of the name of the *serafim*, they can be regarded as 'igneous' powers which stretch out, thanks to their 'wings' or extensions, in all the 'directions' of the cosmos; according to tradition, their holy 'fire' consumes evil and purifies and enlightens created beings. But the essential activity of the *serafim* is the direct affirmation of God; by their 'thrice-holy', they glorify his triple transcendent tri-unity: *kether–hokhmah–binah*, *hesed–din–tifereth*, *netsah–hod–yesod*, and his immanent tri-unity: *shekhinah–metatron–avir*, which is contained in the last *Sefirah*, *malkhuth*. The whole creation is justified and upheld by this praise, as it is by that of all the other created beings; this is why 'the *serafim* are attached to those who sanctify every day the name of their (divine) Master'.

6

In the seventh heaven all manifested things are cosmic 'seeds'; they are in a state of essential fusion, but in no confusion whatsoever; their formal separateness is already prefigured, but not yet consummated. The effective differentiation of created things begins only in the sixth heaven, which is a manifestation of the *Sefirah din*, the universal discernment or 'judgement' of God.

The Talmud (*Hagigah* 12b) calls the sixth heaven *Makhon*, meaning 'place' or 'base', and describes it in the following words: '*Makhon* contains the reserves (of purifying and expiatory manifestations) of snow, hail, harmful dew, round drops fatal to vegetation; its doors are in flames; as it is said (Deuteronomy 28:12): "YHVH will open unto thee his good treasure"'; the manifestations of divine rigour are in reality good, for rigour is nothing other than grace in so far as it denies all negation of God. The sixth heaven, which represents the sphere of universal discrimination, is for man either a treasury of pure mercy or a source of the 'kindness that chastises'; although judgement rules there, this heaven is called 'the palace of mercy' by the Kabbalah; from another point of view, the Kabbalah calls it the 'palace of will', since all the lower spirits wish to be united with the spirit of this palace which is rising towards the supreme spirit in order to become integrated in it. The union of the spirits with their transcendent essence takes place in what the Song of Solomon (1:2) speaks of as the 'kiss of his mouth', signifying beatific absorption in God; Moses died in this divine 'kiss' and not by an ordinary death; it is he who rules in the sixth heaven, which for this reason is also known as the 'palace of Moses'. It is the heaven of the law, which contains both the mercy and the rigour of God; and so it is the prophet of the law who reigns there as *metatron*'s representative.

The spirit of Moses which fills the sixth heaven is truly the spirit of love, for he brings about spiritual union with God in those who have lived in accordance with the law; into his 'palace' only the souls of the 'zealous' may enter, the souls of those who love the Lord truly, who gave praise to the One day after day during their earthly life. Abraham, Isaac and Jacob, although ruling in lower heavens, also have their abode in the sixth heaven; each of them guards one of the 'gates' which at the same time represent

the centre of the fifth, the fourth and the third heaven respectively.[1]
Jacob is in the company of the twelve heads of the tribes of Israel;
whenever Israel is in distress, the three patriarchs implore the
shekhinah to protect its people.

Moses, the patriarchs and the other souls dwelling in the sixth
heaven are surrounded by the four archangels: *Mikhael* ('Who is
like unto God?') *Gabriel* ('strong in God'), *Rafael* ('God has
healed') and *Oriel* (or *Nuriel*, 'light of God'; when he calls men to
return to God, *Oriel* takes the name of *Fanuel*, 'turn towards God!');
the archangels are the principal manifestations of the four *hayoth*[2]
in this celestial 'palace'. While the angels of the seventh heaven
are the hidden motive forces of the cosmos and are revealed to the
prophets and saints only in ecstatic visions – that is to say beyond
all earthly perception – the archangels are apt to assume human
appearance and to manifest themselves to men. Thus, according
to tradition, it was *Mikhael*, *Gabriel* and *Rafael* who appeared to
Abraham in the form of 'three men', when he was sitting at the
entrance to his tent 'in the heat of the day', in Mamre; he received
them, offering them a good meal, 'and they did eat', as it is said
in Genesis (18:1–8). In this story, the Scriptures make it plain that

---

[1] It has already been pointed out above that the prophets can have many
dwelling places in the heavens, in which they manifest different *Sefiroth*
accordingly. In the same way, they may express, on earth, divine aspects other
than those they manifest in heaven, this being the possibility inherent in human
nature itself, which represents the personification of all the *Sefiroth* in created
being, even if only in bodily form, made in the 'image of God'. Thus, from the
viewpoint of their mission on earth – which, according to the law of extremes
which 'meet' reveals the essential quality of each prophet – the Messiah is the
incarnation of *hokhmah*, God's 'wisdom' and redemptive presence; Moses of
binah, his onto-cosmological 'intelligence' and the 'mother' of the law of the
worlds; Abraham, of *hesed*, universal 'grace' or charity; Isaac, of *din*, divine
'judgement' appeased by the sacrifice of man; and Jacob, of *tifereth*, the
'beauty', harmony and union of all the aspects, transcendent and immanent, of
God. The other prophets represent either 'minor' manifestations of the said
Sefiroth, or messengers of the lower *Sefiroth*, not to mention other non-Jewish
prophets, who express the divine qualities in the framework of their respective religion.
[2] Cf. p. 83.

the apparition took place when the patriarch was in the waking state, not in ecstasy, and that the angels were outwardly indistinguishable from ordinary mortals.

The function of the four archangels is to guard over the spiritual and substantial forces flowing from the four 'letters' or divine sources of the name Y H V H, and to stand watch, at the 'four cardinal points' of the sixth heaven, over the lower worlds. As the chief angelic mediators between God and humanity, their principal mission is to bring revelations to the prophets; to direct the prophets and righteous men in their ascent to the heavens; to inspire them in critical moments of their earthly life and to protect them at all times. In fulfilling these functions, the four archangels manifest – as their names imply – different aspects of the celestial influence: *Mikhael*, holiness; *Gabriel*, strength; *Rafael*, charity; *Oriel*, knowledge or, under his attribute *Fanuel*, conversion; besides carrying out their cosmic mission, the archangels 'sing praises in the presence of the Lord of Glory'.

The tradition adds to the four archangels three others whose names vary in the different esoteric and exoteric texts; they are called respectively *Raguel* (who draws down vengeance from the world of the luminaries), *Sarakiel* (in charge of the spirits of children of men who sin against the heavenly spirits) and *Remeiel* (whom God has put in charge of resurrected beings);[1] or *Izidkiel*, *Hanael*, *Kefarel* or else *Tsadkiel*, *Malkhiel* and *Kadmiel*. The function of each of the archangels includes the overseeing of one of the days of the week; *Mikhael*, their 'prince', reigns on the Sabbath, and it is he also who dwells in the centre of the six directions of space, each of which is watched over by one of the other archangels.

The sevenfold function of the archangels becomes, by refraction, that of the seventy 'heads' of the peoples on earth: according to the *Targum jer.* (I Gen. 11:6, 7), God set these seventy celestial princes over the seventy peoples who were established at the same time as the seventy languages, that is, at the time of the building of the Tower of Babel. From that time on, each of

[1] Cf. *The Book of Enoch* (Ethiopian text, xx).

the peoples of the world was guided by a great celestial leader, in accordance with the commands of the supreme King; these angelic leaders are the 'genii' and 'advocates' of the peoples and they are responsible before God for those whom they direct. Thus, according to the *Midrash* (*Shir Rabba*, 27b), the Lord never punishes any one of the peoples without having previously humiliated its guardian angel; in *Tanhuma Beshallah* (13), it is also said that he will not judge the peoples before having judged their heavenly leaders. According to *Pesikta* (176a), it can happen that these angelic governors accuse Israel before God; in that case it is Israel's patron, *Mikhael*, the highest of the archangels, who defends it.

7

The fifth heaven is a manifestation of the *Sefirah tifereth*, 'beauty', or the love of God.[1] The 'seminal' possibilities of *Araboth*, after the cosmic discrimination to which they are subject in the sixth heaven, appear here in their developed state; all the 'separated' heavenly multitude is there united in marvellous harmony and interpenetration under the influence of divine love.

The beings of this heaven are so many vibrations at the same time of light and of sound, myriads of 'waves' each of a different shade of colour and singing praises to the Lord in a different way. All these subtle waves permeate one another so that they actualize the great harmony of heavenly 'sounds' and 'colours' and are finally integrated in the very principle of this unison: the omnipresent One. The human souls who dwell here sing their praises 'while there is daylight on earth', that is, in accord with the prayers rising from here below; and 'during the night', that is to say, during the heavenly phase corresponding to inactivity on earth they are absorbed in the immanent One and blissfully rest therein. Then it is that the angels of the fifth heaven continue to worship 'until morning' – when human activity is resumed – and are

[1] In order to indicate this aspect of love, the Kabbalists often replace the name of the *Sefirah tifereth* by that of *rahamim*, meaning divine 'mercy'.

reabsorbed in God 'during the day'. Thus the Talmud (*Hagigah* 12a), speaking of the fifth heaven, which it calls *Ma'on*, 'dwelling', says: 'In *Ma'on* there are hosts of ministering angels who sing during the night but keep silent during the day in honour of Israel (which is then praising God), as it is said (Psalms 42:9): "In the daytime, YHVH will command his loving kindness (to allow man to affirm him in the waking state), and in the night (in the state of extinction) his song shall be with me."'

According to the Kabbalah, Abraham, 'who is on the right of the supreme spirit', presides over the 'fifth (heavenly) palace', called *Ahabah*, 'love'. The first patriarch devotes himself to uniting this heaven with the divine spirit, 'until the two make only one'. The mysterious relationship between Abraham, the fifth heaven and their common archetype, *tifereth*, divine 'beauty', is expressed in Abraham's words to his wife Sarah (Genesis 12:11): 'Behold now, I know that thou art a fair woman to look upon.' In this 'palace' it is he who represents 'celestial man': he personifies the 'middle pillar' which passes through *Ma'on* in the shape of the 'cherubim's sword' or the 'thunderbolt' of divine knowledge; when this spiritual 'sword' transpierces the fifth heaven, marking the passage of central axis, it appears as a manifestation of divine rigour issuing from *Makhon*, the focus of the Mosaic law. But Abraham, the 'father of a multitude' of peoples, transforms the 'thunderbolt' by means of his universal charity into 'rays of salvation' going forth from the centre of *Ma'on* to the 'four cardinal points' or confines of creation.

The patriarch, who dwells in the 'middle pillar', is surrounded by four *kerubim* or cognitive lights radiating from the 'fiery sword'. These cherubic 'rays' are 'coloured' by the very same divine qualities that are manifested by the four *hayoth* and by the 'four archangels'; they gravitate around their common centre, like the spokes of a wheel, so that the colour of each ray is permeated by those of the others. Through this interpenetration – or union without confusion – of the 'four fundamental colours', all the colours or manifestations of the Sefirothic qualities appear in the fifth heaven in perfect harmony. The four fundamental colours, according to the Kabbalah, are black, white, red and yellow or else green, symbolizing respectively the four 'central' or 'axial' *Sefiroth, kether, tifereth, yesod* and *malkuth*, which synthesize all the others in the 'middle pillar'. Thus *kether*, the supreme and super-intelligible principle, the more-than-luminous darkness, is 'black'; *tifereth*, the mediating and intelligible cause, also called *da'ath*, 'omniscience', the universal light of God, is 'white'; *yesod*, the eternal and common activity of all the *Sefiroth*, God's creative, revelatory and redemptive act, is 'red'; finally, *malkhuth*, his cosmic receptivity, appears 'yellow' or 'golden' like a sun shedding its light over the whole of creation, and 'green' or 'blue' when it is enveloped in *avir*, the ether, and is manifested as eternal and creative substance.

By rotating, the four 'colours' or 'rays' assume the appearance of four 'wheels' (*ofanim*), each of which 'was as it were a wheel in the middle of a wheel'. Thus the four *kerubim*, or spiritual 'shafts of lightning' from *Ma'on*, lose their fiery aspect and are manifested in unitive mode as *ofanim* or celestial 'vibrations'; these are not only vibrations of colour and light, but also of sound, so that their interpenetration gives rise to the 'ocean' of both super-terrestrial 'hues' and also of 'melodies' continually glorifying God in un-speakable harmony and beauty. The 'fifth palace', at first called *Beraka*, 'thunderbolt', changes its name to *Ahabah*, 'love', because of this blissful interpenetration of the 'vibrations' of all the crea-tures with which it is filled; they are all united together and at the same time with the real presence of the One, so that the Scriptures say of this heaven (Song of Songs 7:12): 'There will I give thee my love.'

Thanks to the 'movement of his heart', which encompasses all the 'directions' of the worlds above and worlds below, Abraham changes the 'flaming sword' into a 'wheel' or redemptive vibra-tion; by means of his universal love, he joins all things together and unites them in the One. But what is it which makes a human soul worthy to enter this paradise of beauty, love and unitive adoration? What virtue makes it able to become the patriarch's companion, the companion of 'God's friend' who has the power to raise it up to the supreme spirit? Repentance, or death for God's sake.

8

The cosmic degrees just described represent the 'higher regions' of the heavenly kingdom, where everything is centred solely on affirmation of the Creator and his principal aspects, grace and rigour, and on the synthesis of these, which is his beauty. In those heavens we have now to consider, worship of God does not cease, but at the same time his will corresponds to the behaviour of those created beings who, possessing free will, are able to distinguish between good and evil. In these 'lower regions', the good are rewarded and the wicked punished; there many actions are justified thanks to the intercession of heavenly mediators.

The fourth heaven is a manifestation of *netsah*, divine 'victory', the positive cosmic power. The Talmud (*Hagigah* 12b) calls this heaven *Zebul*, 'dwelling', and says it is 'the dwelling place of the heavenly Jerusalem and of the Temple (on high), where the altar is erected near which stands (the archangel) Michael, the great (celestial) prince, offering a sacrifice upon it, as it is written (I Kings 8:13): "I have surely built thee a house of habitation (*zebul*), a place for thee to dwell in for ever."'

The Kabbalah makes a distinction between two heavenly tabernacles, one situated in the centre of the seventh heaven, the other in the centre of the fourth heaven. The centre of *Araboth* is the spiritual world of *shekhinah–metatron–avir*, the 'heaven of heavens', where the 'original light' of divine immanence 'serves as pontiff' between the transcendence of God and his universal creation. The lower celestial tabernacle is situated at the centre of the fourth heaven, whose 'master' is *metatron*; but here the priestly function is performed by the angel *Mikhael*, the 'great pontiff', ministering between divine immanence and the creatures of the lower heavens and of the earth.

However, the central personification of *metatron* in the fourth heaven is Isaac, the second patriarch of Israel. The question arises why Isaac appears as superior to the great prince and angelic priest, *Mikhael*, why, as 'celestial man', he rules over the altar of *Zebul*. This is so because Isaac accepted the sacrifice of himself to God and thus became worthy to appease the divine wrath; for this reason the second patriarch, 'who stands to the left of the supreme spirit', presides over the 'fourth palace', the seat of justice, from which all the heavenly decrees emanate. Isaac devotes himself to uniting the spirit of 'justification' with the supreme spirit, 'until the two form but one'; the whole of the fourth heaven is filled with this spirit and that is why, in the Kabbalah, *Zebul* is called *Zekhuth*, 'justifying merit.' Isaac's work consists, therefore, in bringing about the absorption of 'justice from which decrees emanate' in 'justification', or the absorption of God's rigour in his grace. Isaac is surrounded by the souls of those who have suffered on earth from the destruction of the Temple, in the cause of the Messiah, or through martyrdom. The Messiah himself leads these souls into Jerusalem and the sanctuary of the fourth heaven in order that *Mikhael* may present them to the Lord as an expiatory offering.

The 'ten great masters of Israel' also dwell in the 'fourth palace', where they contemplate the reverberation of God's single universal light, of which Isaiah (64:3) says: 'Neither hath the eye seen a God beside thee. . . . ' There are also 'seventy lights' in this 'palace'; they compose the 'heavenly tribunal' and above them are two other 'lights' which, as 'witnesses', make this 'higher *Sanhedrin*' complete; and above the *Sanhedrin* are seated four *serafim* – manifestations of the great angelic quaternaries of the upper heavens – from which the 'seventy-two shafts of light' representing the heavenly tribunal are projected; the archetypes of these lights are the 'seventy-two holy names' of God.

9

The third heaven is a manifestation of the *Sefirah hod*, divine 'glory'. It expresses rigorous cosmic power, but is pure grace and light in its centre; God's rigour, as has already been said, is in fact nothing but his grace denying all negation of him; that is why the central manifestations of the third heaven are called *Shehakim*, 'clouds' of grace, while the periphery is 'full of fire and flames'. The Talmud (*Hag.* 12b) speaks only of the beneficent aspects, the *Shehakim*, and calls the third heaven by that name alone: '*Shehakim* is the place of the millstones that grind the manna (or redemptive light) for the righteous, for it is said (Psalms 78:23): "He commanded the skies (*Shehakim*) above, and opened the doors of heaven and he caused manna to rain upon them for food . . ."'

The pure and redemptive light symbolized in the Talmud by 'manna', is called *Nogah*, 'brightness', in the Kabbalah. This is the light of Jacob or of Israel; in its 'colourless' purity, it is neither 'black', nor 'white', nor 'red', nor 'green'. It is the light of absolute monotheism, the reflection of the brightness of the 'One without a second', which eclipses the brilliance or 'colour' of all its aspects: every partial reality, even divine, pales before the One's whole reality and is of necessity extinguished in it. 'This light is called pure because it is free from all mixture' or from all association of a 'second' with the 'One'; but it is 'colourless' only in its centre: in order to communicate with worlds conditioned by diversity, it is compelled to project rockets which, on leaving the centre, take the shape of a sheaf of lights of twenty-two different colours. These are the 'twenty-two celestial letters' of the Hebrew alphabet, the subtle agents of the twenty-two spiritual archetypes which establish all intelligible relationships between the manifestations of the *Sefiroth* in the midst of the cosmos. The twenty-two luminous 'letters' form an indefinite number of combinations, according to the 'movement of the spirit', and draw all the words and all the sentences of the Torah, and finally return, with him who penetrates their meaning, to the single clarity of the One; indeed, the revelation of monotheism, however complex its spiritual doctrines and commandments, emanates in fact from 'simple' unity and returns to that.

Fear of the One makes the third heaven such a pure 'mirror' that its spiritual or angelic manifestations appear analogous to those which occur on the 'surface of the waters'. The 'colourless' light emanating here from the 'middle pillar' is the same as that of the divine throne in *Araboth*; above, it produces the four *hayoth* or supreme angelic beings, as well as the four *ofanim*, 'wheels' or primary cosmic vibrations, and below in the third heaven, it produces 'holy and powerful *hayoth*' and *ofanim* 'the colour of water' – colourless and vibratory – which are none other than the manifestations of those issuing from *Araboth*. Their own fear of God gives rise to an incalculable number of other angels, who praise the Lord and sing hymns to his glory without ceasing. No sooner do prayers from below reach the third heaven than there takes place a fusion of all angels, all spirits and all souls, which is just like the union of all the 'waves' on the 'surface of the waters'; all the beings in the 'third palace' are then united in the spirit which dwells therein and with its pure light, which is the immanent radiance of the One.

Jacob, who is the father of Israel, both according to the flesh, by having engendered the twelve tribes, and according to the spirit, by having given his 'name' or mystical body to the people, represents the perfect and central personification of the pure and unitive light of the third heaven; he is surrounded there by the 'heads of the twelve tribes' and by the souls of those who were afflicted and shed tears during their life on earth because of the destruction of the Temple; the souls of those who suffered greatly on earth on account of grave sicknesses and of those who died before reaching adulthood also dwell in this heaven. The Messiah comes down to console these souls, to bring about their union with the 'middle pillar' and to help them to rise higher.

The light of the 'third palace' does not begin to shine forth until a faint gleam reaches it from below. This is the 'flame from a chip of wood which sets the bonfire ablaze'. The gleam comes from men's prayers; if no prayer rises to heaven, nothing can avert divine judgement and the angels who are known as the 'masters-at-arms' come down to earth to punish mortals. In this case it is no longer the merciful centre but the rigorous periphery of the 'third palace' which prevails; the 'river of fire' (*nahar dinur*) flows on the periphery and in the direction of hell, where it falls on the guilty;

this river is also for the chastisement of angels when they have merited it. The outer or lower 'region' of the third heaven is also the abode of the angels of destruction who torment the damned; these angels, amongst whom is *Samael*, the angel of death, are Israel's accusers; they are the cause of much distress, except when Israel does penance; when it does, these terrible angels have no longer any power over it. In fact the power of repentance is so great that 'if Israel were to repent for one single day, the (Messiah) son of David would straightway be there' (Talmud, P. *Ta'anith* 64a).

10

The second heaven is a manifestation of *yesod*, the cosmic 'foundation' or spiritual and creative irradiation of all the *Sefiroth*. The Talmud (*Hagigah* 12b) calls this heaven *Rakiya*, 'firmament', because the reflections of divine radiation are resplendent there, as it is described symbolically: '*Rakiya* is the support of the sun, the moon, the stars and the planets, as it is said (Genesis 1:17): "God set them in the firmament (*Rakiya*) of the heaven."' Here, therefore, all the lights emanating from the divine aspects are united in the one spirit which the Kabbalah calls *zohar*, 'splendour', or 'brilliant light'. All the keys of wisdom are kept in this heaven and are distributed there to the prophets and sages according to their respective manner of spiritually 'receiving'; and all human souls on their way back to the highest receive here their celestial 'clothing', the appearance of which varies in accordance with the 'merit' they have acquired on earth. The spirits of the prophets and other souls passing through the second heaven are like so many 'stars in the firmament'; the largest and brightest of these luminaries is the spirit of the Messiah 'who stands above them'; he lights up all the souls around him. Amongst these souls are those men who suffered in this world below for their eternal salvation; also the souls of those who gave thanks to God each day, never neglecting their prayer, or who sanctified the holy name with all their strength; these souls ascend from the second heaven towards the highest through the light of the Messiah. As it ascends heavenwards, each soul is led to the 'river of fire' surrounding the third heaven in which it has to be purified: souls which have undergone purification during their life on earth, as well as those whom God pardons, come up out of this river and are clothed in their heavenly raiment; they are then given over to the angelic 'High Priest', *Mikhael*, who presents them, in the tabernacle of the fourth heaven, as a burnt offering to the 'Ancient of Days', and thus causes them to rise towards the divine being. However, it is said that a soul may sometimes drown in the 'river of fire', because its guilt is too great; if so, it is consumed and remains as a flame amongst flames until the end of all the cycles of existence, when hell fire will be extinguished and dissolved in *avir*, the 'very pure and imperceptible air' breathed by the eternal One.

We have just seen that the essential aspect of the 'second palace' is wisdom. The spirit which animates it is the 'white light' of knowledge which makes it possible 'to see in all the directions' of universal reality; this omniscient 'white' spirit is joined with another spirit, 'black' in 'colour' and proceeding from the more than luminous essence of all knowledge. It is this mixture with the 'black' which 'darkens' – or renders unlimited and superintelligible – the 'whiteness', or intelligibility, of the light of the second heaven and transforms it into true wisdom, that wisdom which finally becomes 'more than conscious' identity with the 'nothingness' (*ain*) which is the absolute. From this universal and superintelligible light 'wheels' (*ofanim*) or spiritual vibrations are emitted, as well as seraphic, purifying and sanctifying manifestations; but this 'spiritual movement' does not start only from the divine light immanent in the second heaven; it also comes from 'below', from man. When the sound of his prayer is heard in the heavens, the angels in every 'region' are moved; the *ofanim* or spiritual vibrations of the lower celestial spheres arise and all the other angels try together with them to come nearer to the supreme spirit which gives them life and movement. 'And that bending of the knee (before God) which marks the moment when a man seeks union with his (supreme) master corresponds (here below) to this (spiritual) exaltation.'

II

The first heaven is a manifestation of *malkhuth*, the divine 'kingdom', in its two aspects of spiritual immanence and of substantial principle; this heaven reveals or veils the *shekhinah*, according to which of these aspects predominates in response to the attitude assumed by man 'here below'. The Talmud (*Hagigah* 12b) alludes to this truth when it says of the first heaven that it is called *Vilon* – corresponding to the Latin *velum*, 'veil': '*Vilon*'s only function is to be rolled up in the morning (to make way for the sunlight, symbol of divine irradiation) and to be unrolled in the evening (in order to hide it) as it is written (Isaiah 40:22): "He that stretcheth out the heavens as a curtain and spreadeth them out as a tent to dwell in."'

The Kabbalah also describes the first heaven in these two aspects, the one spiritual or luminous, the other substantial or dark. On the one hand, it is described as the 'seat of faith', or the 'beginning of the mystery of faith': thanks to its translucence, the true prophets had their visions 'as in a mirror without reflections', and the angelic leaders who dwell there are called 'masters of eyes'; on the other hand, says the Kabbalah, the most peripheral or lower 'region' of the first heaven is deprived of all light; there the angels are like hurricanes whose passage is felt but who cannot be seen. They are unconscious of their own existence, because no form exists in their 'region'; they are destroyed every day by imperceptible claps of thunder and are renewed every morning.

These two aspects, intelligible and unintelligible, of the first heaven, are also described – in the 'treatises on the (celestial) palaces' – as 'two spirits': the one, called *Safira* – because 'its light is like that of the sapphire' – is none other than the divine irradiation in the midst of the 'first palace'; the other, called *Lebanah*, 'moon' – because it is purely receptive, 'its lights being only reflections of the lights of *Safira*' – is identical with the ether when it descends to the first heaven. Now it is said that the majority of those who see the light of *Lebanah* coming down from above to shine on them are not aware that in reality this is the irradiation of *Safira*, for *Lebanah* in an imperceptible manner absorbs and veils *Safira*. There are many also who do not know that the more a man purifies his substance and concentrates his mind on the only truth, the more the universal substance – 'ether in the heart' – becomes translucid for him until at last his inner eye sees the divine irradiation without the veil; 'he sees the light of *Safira* directly', whereas others perceive it 'like someone who sees the sunlight reflected by water'. Man reaches direct contemplation of the divine light thanks especially to prayer; when God grants it, 'the light comes down from heaven, surrounds him, rejoices his heart and leads him to contemplate the mysteries . . .'

Prayer not only draws down divine grace upon him who prays but also has a universal repercussion. Thus the 'spirit of the first palace turns its eyes upwards towards the second palace', and its 'vibrations' or *ofanim* are directed towards the *hayoth* or great spiritual manifestations of the second heaven – which, in turn, are directed towards the angels and spirits of the first heaven, and all await the moment when man's prayer will bring about the 'union of all the palaces'; this union takes place in the 'pillar' situated in the middle of the 'lower palace' and rising to the summit of the 'highest palace'. All wise and righteous men, as well as converts, are brought into the 'lower palace' or first degree of the earthly paradise, where they may contemplate the divine mysteries and prepare themselves to rise to the 'first palace' of the heavenly paradise, called *Safira* and presided over by Jacob's well-beloved son Joseph, 'the just'; the 'middle pillar' allows beings to rise – either gradually or directly, according to their state of 'preparation' – to the seventh heaven, which is the celestial 'mystery of mysteries' and where all the cosmic degrees finally become one. All creatures, whether living on earth or sojourning in heaven, should cleave to the 'middle pillar', situated in the centre or 'heart' of their particular existential state, if they wish to be united with the supreme spirit, their common and divine essence, of which it is said in the Scriptures (Ecclesiastes 3:19): 'Yea, they all have one breath.' But, let it be repeated: 'it is man's prayer which brings about the union of the spirit below (immanent in creation) with the spirit on high (the transcendental spirit of God) and through that, the union of all that is'.

v The Corporeal World and the Cosmic Abyss

I

'Thus speaks YHVH: The heaven is my throne and the earth is my footstool.' This verse from Isaiah (66:1) shows the position and the hierarchical relationship of the celestial and terrestrial worlds; it points even more clearly to their common destiny, which is to serve as the spiritual and substantial support for the revelatory and redemptive presence of God.

The divine 'throne' is the first crystallization of all the creatural possibilities. It synthesizes all their spiritual, subtle and corporeal, or prototypical, celestial and terrestrial aspects. This synthetic creation serves as a 'vehicle' for divine immanence; when the *shekhinah* comes down in its 'chariot' to the lower limit of the cosmic expanse, all created things issue from it and open out on their respective existential planes.

The 'throne' is the celestial revelation of the *shekhinah* and God's 'footstool' is his terrestrial radiation; in the heavens, the spirit is revealed through subtle or animic substance, and on earth, not only through this, but in coarse matter also. Our world, therefore, is threefold in nature; it is spirit, soul and body; the *Zohar* (*Vayehi* 231a) is alluding to this when it says, using the symbol of the 'foundation stone' instead of the 'footstool': The foundation stone 'is made up of fire (spiritual light), water (subtle substance) and air (ether, the quintessence of the corporeal elements)'.

The divine 'footstool' or 'foundation stone' is nothing other than the revelation of the supreme tri-unity here below. The material quintessence, the indistinct and unintelligible ether, 'symbolizes' – according to the law of inverse analogy – the indeterminate and superintelligible essence, *kether* or *ain*; the light of the immanent spirit manifests the causal radiation of *hokhmah*; and the subtle substance of the heavens and of souls is the cosmic reflection of divine receptivity, *binah*. Thanks to this correspondence, the 'foundation stone' hidden in the centre or 'heart' of all corporeal things as their synthesis becomes the 'philosopher's stone' for man, through which he contemplates the highest mysteries and thus reaches divine and deifying knowledge.

2

We have just seen how, in esotericism, the symbols divine 'footstool' and 'foundation stone' are identical; when investigating the nature of the corporeal universe, the Kabbalah asks the same question as Job (38:6): 'Whereupon were the foundations thereof fastened and who laid the cornerstone thereof?'[1] The *Zohar* (*Pekude* 222a) replies: 'When the Holy One, blessed be he, was about to create the world, he detached one precious stone from underneath his throne of glory and plunged it into the abyss, one end of it remaining fastened therein while the other end stood out above; and this other and superior head constituted the nucleus of the (corporeal) world, the point out of which the world started, spreading itself right and left and in all directions (of space) and by which it is sustained. That nucleus, that stone, is called *shethiyah* (foundation), as it was the starting-point of the world. The name *shethiyah*, furthermore, is a compound of *shath* (founded) and *Yah* (God), signifying that the Holy One, blessed be he, made it the foundation and starting-point of the world and all that is therein.'[2]

The corporeal universe begins to evolve, therefore, starting from this 'stone' which is its first crystallization, comprised in the synthesis of all creatural possibilities: the 'throne of glory'. God

[1] Another verse from Scripture referring to the 'foundation stone' is to be found in Isaiah (28:16): 'Behold, I lay in Zion (synonym of the centre of the earth) for a foundation a stone, a tried stone, a costly cornerstone of sure foundation.'

[2] The *Zohar* also mentions on this subject (Psalms 118:22): 'The stone (taken from the "throne" and cast into the "abyss") which the builders (that is, the creative causes or *Sefiroth*) rejected is become the chief cornerstone (the divine centre here below).'

broke this 'stone' from his 'throne' and hurled it into the cosmic 'abyss'; then 'one end of it remained fastened therein while the other end stood out above'. This is how tradition teaches that the aggregate of terrestrial possibilities was first plunged into dark 'chaos'; the lower part remained fixed there and the upper part alone – including the possibilities of 'formation' – emerged from chaos in order to become the nucleus of our world.

The Kabbalah thus distinguishes between two cosmogonic phases, that of 'chaos' and that of the *Fiat Lux*. But, as we have just seen, the first creative act was effected in the centre of all worlds before these two phases which evolve on the plane of our world; this act was the instantaneous crystallization of all the existential possibilities, the 'throne of glory', which descends, as the *shekhinah*'s 'chariot', to the very depths of the 'abyss'. The Scriptures speak of this first, central and simultaneous creation of all the worlds in the verse from Isaiah (48:13): 'Yea, my hand hath laid the foundation of the earth and my right hand hath spread out the heavens; when I call unto them, they stand up together.'

When creation passes from the first and synthetic mode to the second and differentiated mode, it no longer develops in the same way on the celestial plane as in the corporeal realm; the evolution of terrestrial possibilities takes place in a way which is analogically inverse in respect to that which takes place 'above'. The six heavens evolve beyond time and space, beginning from *Araboth*, the illuminated 'surface' of the cosmos, whereas the corporeal world opens out in time and space, beginning from the dark and chaotic 'abyss'. The evolution of the earth begins with seven phases of material clarification which end in the *Fiat Lux;* not until this stage of cosmic illumination can the terrestrial possibilities be crystallized 'in detail', in the seven other phases, which are those of corporeal formation: these are the 'seven days of creation' mentioned in the Bible, which end on the 'Sabbath', the phase of the deiform world or earthly Paradise.

Before going into the cyclical aspect of material clarification, we have to consider the corporeal elements as they emerge from the ether, their indistinct quintessence; they proceed from it in exactly the same way as the four subtle elements which are their celestial archetypes; but while the latter spring forth from *avir* as manifestations of light, the corporeal elements emerge in the demonic form of 'shadows', or 'adversaries' of their archetypes. In other words, the elements from 'above' issue from the four *hayoth* or 'supports of the throne', while those from 'below' come out from the 'lower part' of the divine 'footstool'; that is to say, from the chaotic part of the 'foundation stone', the dark, inverse image of the 'throne'. The dark elements express the unintelligible aspect of the ether; they are projected out of it in a single confused mass which fills the 'abyss' of this world. 'Now the earth (the first dark mass of corporeal elements) was (to begin with) unformed (*tohu*) and (later) void (*bohu*: pure form, freed from lack of form, *tohu*)' (Genesis 1:2).

The *Zohar* (*Bereshith* 16a) describes the clarification of the corporeal elements, or their emergence from 'chaos', by explaining the following verse from the first chapter of Genesis: ' . . . and darkness was upon the face of the deep; and the spirit (or wind) of God hovered over the face of the waters'. 'When this (spiritual) wind blew,' says the *Zohar*, 'a certain film ("earth", properly so-called) detached itself from the refuse (chaotic "earth"), like the film which remains on the top of boiling broth when the froth has been skimmed off two or three times. When *tohu* (impure "earth") had thus been sifted and purified . . . similarly *bohu* was sifted and purified (until the element "water" came out from it, for, as the *Zohar* tells us further on, *bohu* is called the "face of the waters"). . . . Then what we call "darkness" (covering the abyss) was sifted, and there was contained in it (the element) fire. . . . When what we call "spirit" (which "hovered over the face of the waters" after having come out from the "abyss" with the other elemental forms) was (also) sifted, there was contained in it a still, small voice (the "voice of YHVH", which mysteriously filled the element air)' (*Zohar, Bereshith* 16a).

And so the elements, having emerged from the dark and unintelligible aspect of the ether, gradually rise, in the process of

clarification and manifestation, towards the translucence of the
ether through which the divinity is revealed; in effect, the higher
element, the air, is the cosmic 'sounding board' of the revealing,
illuminating word of God: As soon as the air issues from the
'abyss' and 'hovers over the surface of the (terrestrial) waters',
the corporeal universe is ready to receive the divine word and,
with it, the great illumination, the *Fiat Lux*. 'And God said: Let
there be light!' (Genesis 1:3).

3

'And there was light.' When God uttered his formatory and redemptive word, it was revealed as the 'light (*avr*) which spreads
out and issues from the mystery of the ether (*avir*)', causing all the
'details' of the material universe to unfold in perfect order and
setting all the terrestrial and astral bodies in harmonious movement. This universal movement is actualized through the intermediary of angelic energies, called 'wheels' (*ofanim*), and their
spiral gravitations, called 'whirlwinds' (*galgalim*); these are the
vibratory and spherical manifestations of the *hayoth*, which themselves issue from the divine word in action, *metatron*. They cause
the subtle and corporeal elements to move out to the confines of
the celestial and terrestrial worlds; at the same time they draw the
worlds into continuous rotation around the 'middle pillar', the
spiritual axis of creation.

The four material elements, penetrated by all the corporeal
forms imprinted on them by the radiation of the *Fiat Lux*, unite
in their sacred movement towards the four cardinal points to
which they respectively correspond. ' . . . these four winds were
then joined to the four elements of the lower world: fire, air,
earth and water. And when these winds and these elements were
thus mingled, the Holy One, blessed be he, formed one body of
wondrous perfection (in the image of the heavenly and spiritual
worlds). Therefore it is plain that the substances composing man's
body belong to two worlds, namely, (the corporeal elements to)
the world below and (the subtle elements and their spiritual or

THE UNIVERSAL MEANING OF THE KABBALAH

Hayothic archetypes to) the world above. Said Rabbi Simeon: 'the first four elements (the subtle elements, the celestial emanations of the *hayoth*, which themselves issue from the four letters of the name YHVH, that is, from the four fundamental aspects of divine all-reality) have a deep significance for the faithful (in the four-fold mystery of faith); they are the progenitors of all (the created) worlds and symbolize the mystery of the supernal Chariot of Holiness. (Thus, when at the moment of the cosmogony the "throne" begins to move and to be transformed into a "chariot", its four "supports" – the *hayoth* – become its "wheels" (*ofanim*) and their "sweat" or substantial emanation is manifested in the form of the four subtle elements with which the heavens are created and from which proceed the four corporeal elements here below). Also the four (material) elements of fire, air, earth and water have a deep significance (the same as that of their celestial models, which derive from the four aspects of YHVH: Y = *kether-hokhmah*; H = *binah*; V = *hesed–din–tifereth–netsah–hod–yesod*; H = *malkhuth*; or again, Y = the "world of (Sefirothic) emanation"; H = the "world of (prototypical) creation"; V = the "world of (celestial) formation"; H = the "world of fact"). From them come gold, silver, copper and iron (the four principal metals) and beneath these other metals of a like kind. Mark well this! Fire, air, earth and water (in their principial state, identical with the four aspects of YHVH) are the sources and roots of all things above and below and on them are all things grounded. And in each of the four winds (which correspond to them, having the same archetypes) these elements are found – fire in the North, air in the East, water in the South, earth in the West; and the four elements are united with the four winds – and all are one. Fire, water, air and earth; gold, silver, copper and iron; north, south, east and west – these make altogether twelve (the figure which symbolizes the complete unfolding of our world and which is manifested on the temporal plane in the form of the twelve signs or constellations of the Zodiac); yet they are all one (the terrestrial world, whose unity – spirit–soul–body – is revealed by man)' (*Zohar, Vaera* 23b, 24a).

4

As soon as 'there was light', all the forms of our world unfolded in the image of their eternal archetypes; all the details of the corporeal universe were finished in the 'six days' or formatory phases which ended on the Sabbath, the seventh cycle, the terrestrial reflection of the immutability and perfection of the creative principle.

The 'seven *Sefiroth* of construction' manifest themselves in the 'seven days of (formative) creation'; but before that they already act on our cosmic plane, during the seven phases of the clarification of the elements, culminating in the *Fiat Lux,* which inaugurates a cycle of perfect balance between spirit and matter. 'God saw that the light was good, and God separated the light from darkness'; he took all obscure matter out of the spirit, in order to shape the matter by the spirit and so to illuminate the darkness in its 'details' during the 'seven days of (formative) creation'.

Now the seven 'previous cycles' or phases of the clarification of matter are mysteriously referred to in the Scriptures (Genesis 36:31-9) as the 'kings that reigned in the land of *Edom* (*ADVM*, the imperfect prefiguration of *ADaM*, the "king" of our world) before there reigned any king over the children of Israel (which in this case means the children of Adam).' According to the Scriptures, seven of these 'kings' died, but not the last one, Hadar, the only one who is said to have had a wife, Mehithabeel. The *Sifra Ditseniutha* (Book of the Arcana) says on this subject: 'Before there was "balance" (cosmic equilibrium established by the harmonious co-operation between the active and spiritual "masculine" principle and the receptive and substantial "feminine" principle) the face (of the spiritual cause) did not look at the face (of the substantial cause); and so these "first kings" (or worlds of elementary clarification preceding the *Fiat Lux*) perished . . . '; and the *Idra Zutta* (the lesser Assembly) comments: ' . . . for the primitive worlds had been made without formation. This is why these unfinished worlds are called "flying flames", "sparks" . . . they could not subsist until the Holy Ancient had made them firm and the Artisan (the divine word) had given a form to his work (by the *Fiat Lux*); he gave it a male and female form (spiritual and substantial, or active and receptive, a double form incarnated in Adam and Eve and "prefigured" by Hadar and Mehithabeel) and, thanks to this, everything subsists (in the midst of the present world), even the extinct "sparks" (from the earlier worlds which were rekindled by the formative illumination of the cosmos).'

These passages from the Kabbalah, and others like them, make it clear that the 'land of Edom' was the same as the world of *bohu* or of the clarification of matter, which issued from *tohu*, the primordial 'chaos'; the 'kings of Edom', called 'flying flames', were subtle or animic manifestations seeking in vain to 'incarnate' themselves in a stable, material form, since coarse substance was still in a state of constant elementary transformation; because of this, they could neither become fixed in it, like souls becoming 'organically' integrated in bodies, nor assimilate it, as we take in food, and so it is said that the 'first kings perished for lack of food'. Only in Hadar and his wife – who represent beings living in the epoch when the 'excess of rigour' had ceased and the clarification of matter had come to an end at the *Fiat Lux* – did spirit and substance come together in a harmonious entity, still, however, lacking a durable form; they prefigured Adam and Eve, or humanity, without attaining the perfection of man, who unites spirit, soul and body in a single stable and symbolic form. It was only during the 'seven days of (formative) creation' following the *Fiat Lux* that all the evanescent configurations of the earlier worlds were resuscitated and moulded into the final forms assumed by the corporeal universe under the influence of the divine word. This re-actualization culminated in the formation of Adam who, just like Hadar who prefigured him, began to reign over the world, now in perfect balance, in the paradisiacal state which prolonged the 'seventh day'.

5

The state of earthly paradise, when peace and harmony reigned between spirit and matter, creator and creation, is called in the Kabbalah the 'upper earth', *Tebel*. Below *Tebel*, there are said to be six other less perfect 'earths', having the semblance of various fragmentary states of the 'upper earth' which, after the 'fall' of Adam, became our own; and in the centre of our "fallen world" remained hidden the first and perfect state of *Tebel*. The tradition concerning the 'seven earths' is common to the *Midrash Esther R.* (I, 12), the *Sefer Yetsirah* (IV, 3) and the *Zohar* (*Sithre Torah,* appendix section *Vayehi*). The 'seven earths' are neither the seven planets—*Shabbathai, Tsedek, Maadim, Hamah, Nogah, Kokhab* and *Lebanah*—nor yet various 'climates', but 'seven countries', hierarchically situated 'one above the other' and 'all inhabited'; seven earthly states, the most perfect of which is that of our earth; their names—*Erets, Adamah, Ge, Neshiah, Tsiah, Arka* and *Tebel*—come from Holy Scripture in which one or another is used to denote the earth.

The eternal archetypes of the seven earths, as of the seven heavens, are the seven *Sefiroth* of construction; but their respective relationship is not as simple and direct as that which exists between the heavens and their transcendent models. The heavens are indeed like seven pure mirrors of the attributes of the Creator, while the earths, with the exception of our own, are more or less tarnished and fragmentary planes of reflection which produce only cloudy and distorted images of the divine causes. *Tebel*, on the contrary, is the whole and perfect symbol of all the *Sefiroth* of construction and man, dwelling on it, is the image of the Sefirothic decade; this is why *Tebel* is said to include, in complete harmony, all the possibilities of the other six earths.

In order to understand the 'becoming' of the seven terrestrial states, we have to go back to the seven phases of the clarification of matter which, as we have seen, culminate in the cycle of the perfect creatural equilibrium actualized by the *Fiat Lux*. This balance comes about gradually and is achieved thanks to the influence of the seven *Sefiroth* of construction, which make order in the elementary chaos; chaos is overcome only at the moment when *malkhuth*, the *shekhinah*, 'comes down' from above, under the aspect of the word of God: amongst all the creative *Sefiroth*, this last one alone takes up its abode in the world below, thereby causing the redemptive light of the 'heavens of heavens' to reign over it.

There is an obvious cosmological relationship between the seven previous cycles or worlds and the seven earths in existence. The reign of the first 'kings of Edom' represents the prototype of the imperfect earths hierarchically situated below *Tebel*. The seven earths are therefore the 'extinguished sparks' or earlier worlds, making their reappearance, but modified now in the light of the human state. However, it should be added that the seven earths represent only one aspect of the re-actualization of the seven previous realms; for the latter were in fact already integrated into all the forms corresponding to them in the midst of the corporeal universe during the 'seven days of creation'. But in so far as the lower terrestrial states aspire to the perfection of *Tebel*, or the human state properly so-called, and are unable to attain it, they re-actualize the earlier states, in which there was the same inability to reach the balanced reign of Hadar or of the *Fiat Lux*.

When the Kabbalah shows the lower earths to be imperfect modes of participation in the human state, it thereby emphasizes the perfection of the latter; the human state is thus seen to be the culmination of a long cyclical and hierarchical development of previous and present terrestrial states. In fact, the human state is not only the end of the evolution of the earth but of the whole cosmogony: it is the 'aim' or 'end' of the work of creation. The 'point on high' becomes the 'point below' in the human state, God's transcendence is revealed therein in the fullness of his redemptive immanence. Man, the 'last to be created', is at the same time the lower synthesis and the most 'explicit' symbol of divine all-reality; in the midst of creation, God knows himself most perfectly through the micro-macrocosmic person of man, and the whole of creation will be reintegrated into the supreme origin through man as intermediary.

6

Above, the seven earths culminate in the earthly Paradise, which is situated in the spiritual centre of *Tebel*. The earthly Paradise

itself has seven degrees, rising from *Tebel* up to the realm of the
heavenly Paradises; these seven 'regions' in the 'lower Eden' thus
represent states intermediate between the corporeal universe and
the subtle or celestial world. Now, in the expanse between the
'earth' and the 'heavens' there are also the 'seven hells', like so
many 'shadows' or dark inversions of the seven earthly Paradises.
The Paradises rise up from the 'snow' – the ether – crowning the
summit of the earthly 'mountain', towards the 'waters' – the
subtle substance – of the heavens; the seven hells, on the contrary,
are the 'abodes of impurity', the chaotic 'mixture' of heavenly
'water' with 'snow', or quintessence of matter. This 'mixture' is the
confused mass in *tohu*, the 'darkness filling the abyss', actualizing
that is, the lower boundary of the cosmos, extreme and illusory
negation of divine infinity. The spirit of 'darkness' is Satan, God's
and man's 'adversary' or 'enemy', the 'counterfeit' of divine
immanence, the other 'lower point' which in truth is the cosmic
'falling-point'. Satan reigns in the substantial 'nest of filth' which
is neither clarified in the pure 'water' of heaven, nor crystallized
in corporeal matter; in other words he is the entity of unformed,
chaotic and demonic elements which fill the 'abyss' of hell.

Let it be made clear that hell, or the world of *tohu*, is situated
below the seven degrees of clarification of matter, which are the
'earlier worlds'; the latter did indeed issue from *tohu*, but they
actually belong to the realm of *bohu*, the realm of the formation of
the elements. Although hell is identical with 'chaos', nevertheless
a kind of hierarchy of states or degrees can be distinguished here;
this hierarchy is the last reflection of the cosmic order, projected
into the midst of the primordial disorder of nature. There, the
formative radiation of the spirit barely touches created being; but
nothing could possibly exist without having been conceived and
'touched' by that spirit and without possessing an eternal archetype. And so even the seven hells are manifestations of the seven
creative *Sefiroth*, but they are dark manifestations, 'shadows' or
inverse images of their luminous, transcendent models. If chaos
were not an inversion of divine order, it would be lacking any real
cause, or in other words it would be nothingness purely and

simply; but this cannot be, since, by existing, nothingness would cease to be nothingness.

The dark reversal of the divine order implies the possibility of a return from chaos, of 'inversion of the inversion', which will be the reintegration of the seven hells in their first, Sefirothic causes. But until this final reabsorption, identical with that of the whole of creation, the hells will contribute, in their negative way, to the maintenance of the cosmic order. In order fully to understand the negative role of 'evil' or Satan, we have to return to the 'cause of causes'. This is pure and infinite reality, filled with bliss; now, the characteristic of happiness is to become aware of itself and to affirm itself and such an affirmation necessarily has to be actualized in the midst of divine all-reality. Thus *kether* is affirmed by *hokhmah*, its luminous emanation, and by *binah*, in receiving its light; this first and ontological affirmation is affirmed in turn by its radiation or creative manifestation, which is originally pure 'grace', *hesed*. In the same way, the cosmic possibilities issuing from divine grace affirm themselves; but by being attached to existential happiness, they forget the pure and divine affirmation, the cause and very sense of their existence. Their affirmation of themselves degenerates into negation of their transcendental essence, and divine grace is obliged to assume the aspect of rigour in order to deny this negation of God. *Din*, 'judgement' of all things issued from *hesed*, sets a limit to cosmic affirmation; this limit is the death of created beings and hell. Death and hell are the realms where Satan's negative spirit reigns, which is called *Yetser hara*, the 'evil inclination' which, from the beginning, was concealed in the affirmation of themselves by created beings and took them further and further from their uncreated source. 'Satan, *Yetser hara* and the Angel of Death are one and the same' says the Talmud (*Baba bathra*, 16a).

The 'evil inclination', which goes down, separates and limits, was enclosed from the beginning in the 'good inclination', *Yetser tob*, which rises towards the highest and affirms it in all things; this relationship between the two opposite tendencies is merely a manifestation of the relationship between rigour and grace, for the first, from which all negation emanates, is eternally comprehended in the second, which is the cause of all affirmation. God himself wishes the existence of the limited cosmos in the midst of his own unlimitedness; and in order to create the finite, he prefigured it by denying himself, by 'contraction' (*tsimtsum*) in the midst of his immutable infinity. Satan was born from this 'contraction' or illusory negation of God, which, in its static aspect, is none other than the *Sefirah*, *din*, divine 'judgement' or rigour. So, if *din*, in cosmic manifestation, at first appears as a negation of the infinite, its true purpose is to negate negation and thus affirm the only reality. In God himself, this aim is achieved eternally; for, in denying himself by *tsimtsum*, God is denying his own negation by his infinity, so that in truth his 'contraction' or denial is purely illusory. The denial of God only becomes apparently concrete in the 'cosmic mirage', preceding the 'negation of the negation' which reabsorbs all limits into the infinite. Man was created with these 'two tendencies' in order that he might deny the negation of God by affirming God and thus overcome evil with good and reconcile all existential opposites in deifying union. When, in the 'world to come', man will have carried out this work, then, says the Talmud (*Sukka*, 52a), 'the Holy One, blessed be he, will call *Yetser hara* to appear before him and will cause him to perish . . . .'.

Until then, every time man causes God's wrath to overflow, 'darkness' will fill the 'abyss' and the chaotic elements will appear upon the earth in order to carry out their destructive work. Satan will continue to play the role of 'tempter', and 'angel of death', concerning himself with man even beyond the grave; the human soul which chooses *Yetser tob*, the 'good (and upward) tendency' in its way through earthly life will rise, thanks to it, towards God, but the soul wedded to *Yetser hara*, the 'bad (and downward) tendency', will go to hell with Satan.

The fall of the soul from our divinely ordered world into the darkness of the 'abyss' is due to its sins against the reign of the Holy One, in which it was graciously allowed to participate during its life on earth; such sins and the consequent fall can only be annulled by *teshubah*, 'repentance' before death, which calls for God's forgiveness. By his revelation, God gives man knowledge of the universal law, so that he may conform to it and consciously take his place in the order of the worlds; what is more, since this order manifests the wisdom and other perfections of the Creator, man, by submitting to the higher law, can in principle have access to these sublime qualities and become absorbed, by the way of spirit and of grace, in the One who is clothed in these qualities. In any case, having received the gifts of discriminative intelligence and of a relatively free will, man is responsible for his attitude towards the will of God; he is judged according to this when his life on earth is consummated.

7

' . . . in quitting this world a man has to endure seven ordeals. The first is the judgement of heaven when the spirit leaves the body. The second is when his actions and utterances march in front of him and make proclamation concerning him. The third is when he is placed in the grave. The fourth is the ordeal of the grave itself. The fifth consists in his being consumed by the worms. The sixth is the suffering endured in Gehenna (which every soul has at least to "taste" when being purified in *nahar dinur*, the subtle "river of fire"). The seventh ordeal is that his spirit is condemned to roam to and fro in the world, and is not able to find a resting place until his appointed tasks have been completed. (This is the punishment which Kabbalists call *gilgul*, the "transmigration" of the soul, by which grave faults and omissions committed during earthly existence must be repaired.) Hence it behoves man continually to review his actions and to repent before his Master. When David reflected on these ordeals which a man has to endure he made haste to exclaim: "Bless the Lord, O my soul, and all my inward parts, bless his holy name" (Psalms 103:1), as much as to say: "Bless the Lord, O my soul, before thou quittest the world, whilst thou still inhabitest the body; and all my inward parts, all the members of the body that are in union with the spirit, whilst this union still lasts, hasten to bless his holy name, before the time comes when you will not be able to bless or repent"' (*Zohar, Vayak'hel* 199b).

This is why the 'Treatises of the Palaces' praise the lot of him who 'is able to shelter from the bad side and all the steps leading from it', for, as they say, the spirit of temptation has various 'degrees' or aspects, and this is confirmed by the Talmud where they are called: the 'coiled serpent' (identical with the 'evil inclination', *Yetser hara*); Satan (the 'adversary' of God and man) and the 'exterminating angel'. In connection with these three fundamental aspects, the Devil has seven names: Satan, the impure, the enemy, the stumbling-block, the uncircumcised (in the sense of bestiality), the evil one, the sly one. These seven names correspond to the 'seven palaces of the side of impurity', which are the seven stages of hell where the punishment of guilty souls takes place after death; just as on the 'holy side', the side of Paradise, there are also seven 'palaces' on the 'impure side', in hell, which are the dark inversions of the heavenly 'palaces' and they are called: well, precipice, silence of the tomb, guilt, *Sheol*, shadow of death, and lower earth. These seven infernal states are like the links of a chain, the beginning of which is joined to the end.[1] This being so, the 'first palace' is situated on the 'upper boundary' of the 'demon's empire'; the 'second palace' is darker than the first, and in the third, 'darkness reigns with the greatest intensity', so that from this point in the process of falling it seems as though the steps of hell are leading upwards towards the surface of the 'abyss'; nevertheless, the 'sixth palace' is worse than the others, while the seventh leads back to the upper boundary of hell, through 'windows opening onto the Empire of holy Light'. Such are the 'seven palaces' of the 'impure spirit', about which the Kabbalah says: 'In time to come (the moment of universal redemption) God will cause it to disappear from the world, as it is written (Isaiah 25:8): He will swallow up death forever; the Lord Y H V H will wipe away tears from off all faces. . . . '

[1] This circular arrangement of the degrees of hell has its archetype in that of the Sefirothic hierarchy, the 'end of which meets the beginning'; *malkhuth*, the last *Sefirah*, which is identical with the *shekhinah*, divine immanence, is eternally united with *kether*, the supreme principle.

VI The Mystery of Man

I

' . . . in the beginning, before shape and form had been created, he (God) was without form and similitude. . . . But when he had created (supraformally and prototypically) the form of supernal man it was to him as a chariot (support of immanence), and he descended (from supra-intelligible transcendence) on it, to be known. . . . '

The *Zohar* (*Bo* 42b) is speaking here on the one hand about God in essence and on the other hand about God in action. First it views divine being as it is when hidden in supra-being, the 'mystery within mystery', or non-acting cause in absolute non-cause; this is the universal principle, apart from any relationship with creation, the indeterminate principle which cannot be known. The *Zohar* goes on to consider God as the active cause, radiating the archetypes or principal 'figures' of all created things, these archetypes being none other than the indivisible unity of his being, yet appearing through the Sefirothic 'prism' as so many aspects of himself.

Given that the aspects of divine being constitute both the causes and the 'models' of his cosmic manifestations, there follows an analogical relationship between the latter and their eternal origin: they represent his symbolic 'reflections'. This symbolism makes it possible to contemplate the ontological principle on the level of created things, which are 'images', more or less perfect, of necessary being. Now, the 'image of God' *par excellence* is man, whose integral being alone includes all cosmic realities and their uncreated archetypes. There is no other creature which manifests the totality of the *Sefiroth* so synthetically and at the same time so explicitly as man; he alone incorporates the 'figure of the all' – the universal prototype in its wholeness – whereas other created beings and things, be they the angels, the heavens or the earth in its entirety, only partially express the divine being in one or another of his aspects.[1] The 'figure of the all' *in divinis* is man's own archetype, his uncreated being: 'Man above' (*adam ilaah*); whereas the 'image of the all' is his cosmic manifestation, his created being: 'man below'.

God created the world and all that exists in contemplating 'man above', who is none other than the infinite unity of the ten *Sefiroth*. He created everything in the image of 'man', for he wished to be glorified by the 'mystery of man'; he wished man everywhere, above and below, to be his expression, his revelation, his symbol; and so he gave 'man above' dominion over the whole of his uncreated emanation, and to 'man below' – in so far as he existed in primordial perfection – dominion over the whole of created manifestation. All that exists aspires, consciously or otherwise, to become integrated into the universal and divine being of man, who links the lowest world with the supreme 'self' of all things; and God has given to each thing, according to its particular ability, the power to rise, through manifold transformations, up to the integral 'form' of man, which is the archetype of all archetypes: divine being.

But the totality of 'man above' surpasses even being; it goes beyond the supreme prototype, for it is none other than the transcendence of God in his two aspects, causal and non-causal: his being and his supra-being. The essence of transcendent man is *ain*, the 'nothingness' which is the absolute; and his prototypical 'form' or 'figure' is *ehyeh*, causal 'being'. In order to express the fact that there was no creation so long as God was at rest in the non-cause and was no manifesting in his causal aspect, tradition says that 'the celestial fountainhead did not gush forth over the

[1] It could be objected here that *metatron*, the supreme 'angel', manifests spiritually all the ontological aspects. This is true, but, as we shall see later, 'angel' is only a comparative designation of *metatron*, which derives from the fact that he is pure spirit: the cosmic intellect. Now this is not in any sense a 'separate intelligence', passive and created, like the angels, but is the active, ordering aspect of divine immanence itself, from which it cannot be separated. In reality, therefore, it is uncreated and appears in the form of cosmic totality only through its 'envelope', *avir*, the ether, or substantial cause of creation.

world, because man was hidden in *ain*'. But when man emerged from the supreme 'nothingness' he took on the aspect of Sefirothic emanation, transcending all cosmic form and semblance; and from this 'man of emanation, without image and without likeness', the celestial fountainhead of truth and life gushed forth.

2

In essence, transcendental man is the supreme self, nameless, without any aspect, eternally hidden in himself; and in action he is the sun of divine knowledge, contemplating all intelligible lights in his single clarity and creating all things from his undifferentiated sparks; although myriads of creatures proceed from him, he remains the eternal One. From the viewpoint of the symbolism of the spiritual, psychic and corporeal aspects of man, he is the unity of the *Sefiroth*. His 'hidden brain', the contents of which are not and never will be known, is nothing other than his pure essence, *kether*, the divine 'crown', the supreme and superintelligible principle. His 'right brain' is his ontological 'wisdom', *hokhmah*, through which the One contemplates himself and nothing but himself. His 'left brain' is his onto-cosmological 'intelligence', *binah*, which he uses at the same time as a 'mirror' in which to contemplate his pure unity and as a 'prism' in order to see his unity in all his universal possibilities and all his possibilities in his unity; from this vision there flows the irradiation of the cosmic multitude, the creative emanation. These three 'brains' of transcendental man are also called the 'three heads which are but one', that is, *kether–hokhmah–binah*. His 'right arm' is his incommensurable 'grace', *hesed*, divine mercy; his 'left arm' is his 'rigour', the measure of all things, *din*, universal judgement. His 'heart' or 'trunk' is *tifereth*, supreme 'beauty', or divine love, the fullness, harmony and union of all uncreated and created possibilities. His 'right thigh' is his positive cosmic power, *netsah*, divine 'victory'; and his 'left thigh' is his negative cosmic power, *hod*, the 'Glory' of the Lord. His 'male generative organ' is his eternal, creative and redemptive act, *yesod*, the 'Foundation' of the worlds. Lastly, his 'feet' or 'feminine' aspect are his universal receptivity, *malkhuth*, the 'kingdom', the uncreated receptacle of the divine emanations and the immediate principle of cosmic manifestation.

Although this 'form' of transcendental man is, in itself, 'devoid of aspect and semblance', it produces lights and distinct forms which are 'reflections' or symbolic 'images' of it; and therein lies the whole work of creation, composed of the three worlds – spiritual, subtle and corporeal – and synthesized in the three analogous aspects which together make up 'man below'. In fact, if the supreme tri-unity or 'triple head', *kether–hokhmah–binah*, represents man's pure essence, then the triad *hesed–din–tifereth*, or the two 'arms' and the 'trunk' of *adam ilaah* are the causes and archetypes of the human spirit, as well as of the spiritual world; the human soul, and also the subtle world, proceed from *netsah–hod–yesod*, his two 'thighs' and 'male generative organ'; and the human body and the whole corporeal world issue from *malkhuth*, his 'feet' or 'feminine part'. Thus, 'man below' and the whole of creation are made 'in the image and likeness' of 'man above', who is none other than God.

If 'man above' is the whole of divine transcendence, then strictly speaking, 'man below' is only human individuality, which includes the corporeal and psychic realms. Between the individual plane and the supreme and transcendental plane, there lies the spiritual world, wherein dwells the divine immanence alone; and it is in that that the third fundamental aspect of man is to be found, connecting his created being with his uncreated essence; this is supra-individual and cosmic man. Indeed, after issuing from the supreme mystery and its first emanation, in which he is revealed as *hokhmah*, the eternal wisdom, whence all the other divine irradiations spring, 'man above' is first manifested on the purely spiritual plane. This first manifestation, transcending all form and all individuation, and encompassing all created things like a 'sphere whose centre is everywhere and whose circumference is nowhere', is *metatron*,[1] immanent and universal man.

---

[1] The etymology of this mysterious name is much debated. Its origin has been sought by some in the Hebrew word *nator*, 'to watch over', in the Latin word *metator*, 'one who measures', and in *mater*, 'mother', or *matrona*, the

Metatron is identical with the prototypical 'world of creation' (*olam haberiyah*), filled with the *shekhinah* alone; the latter is the undifferentiated, omnipresent immutable immanence of the ten *Sefiroth* or 'man above'. It is manifested through *metatron*, who is its cosmic act and purely spiritual 'measure', by means of which it determines the forms of all created things; however, the twofold spiritual and immanent principle, *shekhinah–metatron*, would be unable to produce the created forms without the help of the substantial principle, *avir*, the universal and undifferentiated ether, which is the mysterious 'circumference' of the spiritual world. This 'circumference', while existing, is nevertheless 'nowhere' to be found, that is to say it is beyond space and every other cosmic dimension; it is the supreme, unlimited 'firmament', which overhangs creation and constitutes the plane of reflection onto which *metatron* projects light and where his sparks take on form and body. These 'sparks' are the immanent archetypes or spiritual 'seeds' of everything existing in the heavens and on the earth. *Metatron* is their general and undifferentiated 'figure', the only creative and redemptive irradiation of the *shekhinah*; and *avir* is the 'precious stone' through which this undifferentiated light of God appears as the fullness of manifestable possibilities.

The prophet Ezekiel contemplated the immanent plenitude of God through *avir*; it was revealed to him as 'celestial man' or *metatron*, seated on the divine throne. 'And above the firmament that was over their heads was the likeness of a throne (metacosmic elevation), as the appearance of a sapphire stone (symbol of *avir*), and upon the likeness of the throne there was a likeness as the appearance of a man (*metatron*, who dwells) upon it above (creation, in the world of divine immanence). And I saw as it were a shining surface (*ein hashmal*, which can also be translated

---

divine 'lady', which is a descriptive term for the *shekhinah*. Others have supposed it to be derived from the Greek *meta thronon*, 'beyond the throne'; or finally, it has been considered as originating from the numerical value of *metatron*, which is that of the divine name, *Shaddai*, the 'Almighty', of whom metatron is in effect the direct and universal manifestation.

as 'burning eye, or look' and which signifies the universal or all-penetrating consciousness of *metatron*), as the appearance of fire (divine light, shining) round about enclosing it (the spiritual world or *metatron*), from the appearance of his loins and upwards (the upper 'part' of *metatron*, which is united with the divine immanence and through this with the divine transcendence) and from the appearance of his loins and downward (the lower 'part' of *metatron*, which is united with *avir*, pure substance, and through it with creation) I saw as it were the appearance of fire and there was brightness round about him. As the appearance of the bow (the symbol of the principial 'form' of *metatron*) that is in the cloud (symbol of *avir*) in the day of rain (at the moment when the *shekhinah* is revealed or manifested), so was the appearance of the brightness (the universal radiation) around about (the spiritual world, whose omnipresent centre is the *shekhinah* and whose measure or incommensurable form is *metatron* and whose mysterious circumference is *avir*). This was the appearance (*avir*) of the likeness (*metatron*) of the glory (*shekhinah*) of YHVH (which encompasses all the *Sefiroth*, all the aspects of man above)' (Ezekiel 1:26-28).

3

Metatron is God in action; that is why tradition calls *metatron* the 'small YHVH', or universal manifestation of the 'great YHVH', or again 'prince of the (divine) face' (*sar hapanim*), the first revelation of the *shekhinah*. He is the 'angel' or 'messenger' (*malakh*) *par excellence* of God, that is, the whole of God's spiritual descent, through which the totality of his emanations is realized in the world; he is the great universal mediator. God is speaking of *metatron* when he says to Moses (Exodus 23:20): 'Behold, I send an angel before thee to keep thee by the way and to bring thee in to the place which I have prepared. Take heed of him and hearken unto his voice; be not rebellious against him for he will not pardon your transgression; for my name (or total emanation) is in him.' According to the Talmud (*Sanhedrin* 38b), *metatron* is also he who (in Exodus 24:1) commands Moses to go up towards God: 'And unto Moses he said: Come up unto YHVH . . .' Concerning this mediatory function in which *metatron* manifests the divine all-mightiness, the *Midrash Numbers Rabba* (XII) says: 'At the moment when the Holy One, blessed be he, commanded Israel to build the sanctuary, he gave an order to the angels who were present to build another one on their side. The latter is the sanctuary of the 'strong man', called *metatron*; in this (heavenly) sanctuary he offers up the souls of the devout in atonement for Israel during the days of its exile.'

Metatron, who is the supra-formal and purely spiritual 'form' from which issue the forms of all created things, is at first called by the name 'man', and only later receives such secondary epithets as 'wheel' (*ofan*, archetype of all the worlds) or 'angel' (*malakh*, archetype of all celestial beings);[1] this is because, of all created beings, man alone is fit to transform himself spiritually, in a conscious and active way, into *metatron*, who is his own immanent prototype, of which the other cosmic archetypes are only 'aspects'. This possibility of the spiritual transformation of individual man into supra-individual and universal man is confirmed by tradition in the account of the ascent of Enoch to heaven where he became *metatron*.

In the following passages, the *Zohar* alludes to the mystery of the metamorphosis of the individual being into the universal being of man: 'Of the creation of (individual) man the Scriptures say

---

[1] *Metatron* is also called the divine 'scribe'. He writes all the creative thoughts of God in the 'book' or 'world of creation'. His 'pen' is the 'middle pillar' along which flows the luminous 'ink' of divine emanation, descending from the triple 'brain', *kether-hokhmah-binah*, as omniscience (*da'ath*) and then accumulates in the fullness of the *shekhinah* and is engraved on the pure and translucent 'parchment' of *avir*, the generative ether. Everything that was, is and shall be is written in the divine book of *metatron* in the form of 'heavenly letters' or spiritual archetypes. Furthermore, he is known as the 'young man' or eternal 'adolescent' because he is the first, incorruptible and supra-temporal manifestation of divine immanence. In particular he is the first revelation of divine wisdom in regard to the cosmos, the sourse of all orthodox inspiration, the 'master of all the teachers of the Mishnah (oral tradition)'.

(Job 10:11): "Thou hast clothed me with skin and flesh, and hast fenced me with bones and sinews! What, then, is man? Does he consist solely of skin, flesh, bones and sinews? Nay, the essence of man is his soul; the skin, flesh, bones and sinews are but an outward covering, the mere garments, but they are not the man. When man departs (from this world) he divests himself of all these garments (and his soul continues to live beyond the corporeal plane)' (*Jethro* 75b, 76a). ' "And YHVH *Elohim* took the man and put him in the garden of Eden to cultivate it and to dress it" (Genesis 2:15). From whence did he take him? He took him (that is, his body) from the four elements which are hinted at in the verse (Genesis 2:10): '. . . and from there it (*avir*, ether, the indistinct 'quintessence' of the four elements) parted and became four heads.' God detached him from these (four elements, by reintegrating them in the ether which dwells in his heart and envelops his soul in a homogeneous, translucent and undifferentiated way; freed from corporeal conditions, his soul then rediscovers its supra-individual or universal 'form', *metatron*) and (God) placed him in the Garden of Eden (the 'world of [spiritual] creation', filled with the *shekhinah* alone). So does God do now to any man created from the four elements when he repents of his sins and occupies himself with the Torah' (*Zohar Bereshith* 27a). We are concerned, actually, not only with the four corporeal elements, but also with the four subtle or psychic elements which make up human individuality, namely: *nefesh* (literally: 'vitality'), the 'animal soul'; *ruah* (literally: 'air' or 'wind'), the 'mental soul'; *neshamah* (literally 'breath'), the spiritual 'sacred soul'; and *hayah*, the (eternally) 'living soul'. These four elements issue from one single undifferentiated 'quintessence': *yehidah*, the 'one (divine) soul'; their macrocosmic counterpart is in the four *hayoth* or 'living (and angelic) beings' of Ezekiel's vision, who are commanded by the chief (*metatron*, their common principle), who bears the name of the Master: *Shaddai* (the 'all-powerful'). Now when, in man's spiritual transformation, the four corporeal elements are reintegrated in *avir*, then the four psychic elements, in mounting repercussion, in their turn withdraw into *yehidah*, the 'one soul', which, in its substantial nature, is identified with ether, and in its spiritual nature, with *metatron*, and through it with the *shekhinah*. That is why it is said that: 'When man has observed the law, he will govern the four (corporeal) elements (and their immediate, subtle or psychic causes) which are transformed into one (single) river (one single divine emanation: *shekhinah–metatron–avir*), by which his thirst will be quenched (on every level – spiritual, subtle and corporeal – of his manifested being).'

By detaching individual man from the four corporeal elements and their subtle causes, that is, by reinfolding all his individual differentiation into his simple centre, God transforms him into the supra-individual or universal man, whose 'body' is *avir*, whose 'soul' is *metatron*, and whose 'spirit' is the *shekhinah*. If God is the first cause of this transformation, man is its second cause: through study and observation of the revealed law, which leads him to 'penitence', that is, to the recalling of all his individual possibilities into their common and divine centre, he co-operates actively in the process of being made universal and 'sanctified'. This is what is called spiritual concentration on God, in which man brings about the union of corporeal and subtle elements in the one divine immanence: it is the absorption of his five bodily senses and the recollection of his differentiated soul into their unique essence in the heart of his being; and with the help of God, this 'union below' brings about the 'union above', the union of immanent being with transcendent being.

Since the union of man with God takes place through the mediation of the 'real presence', this union, from the point of view of method, is sometimes regarded as a divine 'descent' into the human being, and sometimes as an 'ascent' towards the 'most high'. In both cases, Jewish mysticism includes 'ways of union' which are varied and based primarily on the invocation of the divine names, with all that this implies in the way of purifying preparation, meditation and concentration. To cite but one of these methods, we shall mention the one known as the 'vision of the (divine) chariot': as we have pointed out, the 'chariot' (*merkabah*) is the support for immanence, which allows God, by way of emanation, to 'descend' into the cosmos, and to 'reascend' by reintegration into himself; seen 'from within', the 'chariot' is the *shekhinah* itself, and seen 'from without' it is its substantial envelope, *avir*, the ether, hidden in the heart, and uplifting the soul through the seven created heavens or celestial 'palaces' (*hekhaloth*) to the 'heaven of heavens', the spiritual and proto-typical 'world of creation'; there, the soul recovers its universal 'form', *metatron*, and is united with the *shekhinah*, seated on the 'throne' or 'chariot' at rest. The initiates in this method of 'ascent' are named 'those who descend in the chariot' (*yorde merkabah*) because the initiate has to 'descend' to the innermost depth of his heart where the ethereal 'chariot' is hidden, ready to raise him through all the heavens towards the divine world.

Every ascent from one celestial degree or 'palace' to another calls for a 'descent', and adequately deep 'probing' of the heart, that is, the realization of a spiritual virtue or quality which reflects a particular divine aspect, ruling a particular celestial 'palace'. According to a treatise on the *hekhaloth*, Rabbi Akiba said to Rabbi Ishmael (two great Kabbalistic masters and *yorde merkabah*): 'When I ascended to the first palace, I was devout (*hasid*), in the second palace I was pure (*tahor*), in the third, sincere (*yashar*: upright, just, fair), in the fourth I was wholly with God (*tamim*: perfect, spotless, faultless), in the fifth I displayed holiness before God, in the sixth I spoke the *Kedushah* (the 'thrice holy . . .') before him who spoke and created (the world), in order that the guardian angels might not harm me; in the seventh palace I held myself erect with all my might, trembling in all my limbs, and spoke the following prayer: Praise be to Thee who art exalted, praise be to the Sublime in the chambers of grandeur!'[1]

Enoch, like Moses and Elijah, figures in the sacred history of Israel among many other prophets and saints who, whether in their spiritualized body or only in their soul – the body remaining as it were lifeless on earth – have achieved the celestial 'ascent' which ends in the union of man with God.

[1] Quoted from: *Major Trends in Jewish Mysticism*, by G. G. Scholem (New York, Schocken Books, 1961), pp. 78–9.

4

The human soul, in the supra-individual totality in which it is one with *shekhinah–metatron–avir*, the immanent triple principle, dwells beyond all the created heavens in the prototypical 'world of creation'. It is the divine light which completely fills this 'sphere, whose centre is everywhere and whose circumference is nowhere', in the words of the Scriptures (Proverbs 20:27): 'The soul of man is a light of YHVH.' The soul, in descending into the earthly body, moves away from its universal form and is transformed, by individualization, into the soul of some particular man, but it remains connected with the total soul, which is divine, through a spiritual 'ray'. By means of this 'ray', *metatron*, the universal and active spirit, directs the human individual according to the will of God, while leaving him his share of free-will granted by the Lord Most-High; and it is thanks to this same 'ray' that the soul, when it comes to be transformed, rediscovers the path which brings it back to its origin.

Transcendent man, *adam ilaah*—also called *adam kadmon* ('principial man') – is God in his essence and his ontological emanation; immanent man, *metatron*, is God's whole spiritual manifestation; and earthly man, *adam harishon* ('first man') is his manifestation, at one and the same time above form (spirit), in subtle form (soul) and in coarse form (body), that is, his cosmic personification, which is identified both with the universal realm and – in the midst of it – with the individual state. Whereas *adam ilaah*, divine man, and *metatron*, his purely spiritual manifestation, represent invariable principles, the first man, in the historical sense, is already subject to the movement of existential and cyclical conditions; but it must be pointed out that this is so only as regards his individual aspect, 'man below', and to the extent that he dissociates himself from his inner, universal and incorruptible being, *metatron*, and by that very fact from 'man above', who is one with God. This dissociation is the 'original sin' which caused the first man to lose his state of permanent union with God and led him into the movement of individual existence, unfolding through countless births and deaths.

The *Zohar* describes transcendental man as follows (*Terumah* 144b): 'The holy supernal man rules over all and gives (spiritual and substantial) food and (eternal and transitory) life to all.' Of immanent and universal man it says (*Mishpatim* 105a): 'The Holy One, blessed be he, has a son (a manifestation) whose glory shines from one end of the world to another. He is a great and mighty tree, whose head reaches (the highest) heaven (the Sefirothic world, source of all spiritual light) and whose roots are set in the holy ground (*avir*, universal ether, cause of all substance).' Finally, the *Zohar* (*Bereshith* 34b) speaks of the creation of the first terrestrial man and describes how the four cardinal points came together and said to one another: 'Let us make a man in our image, after our likeness, embracing like us the four quarters (of space) and the higher and the lower.' Now, the six directions of space reflect all the supra-spatial expansions of the subtle world, and all the spiritual 'dimensions' of the world of divine immanence. In effect, God has given the body, soul, and spirit of man co-extensibility with the three corresponding worlds, which co-extensibility manifests the infinity of 'man above'. Thus, the 'first (synthetic) body' of man is none other than the ether which fills the whole of space; his 'first (supra-individual) soul' is in the macrocosmic form of all creation; and his superhuman and universal spirit is in the prototypical 'form' of *metatron*. In other words beginning from the earthly state, in which his 'second (differentiated) body' explicitly symbolizes Sefirothic unity, up to the supreme state in which he is that unity itself – 'the figure of the all' – man, in the perfection of his multiple states, has within him complete form of every fundamental degree of existence. That is why the *Zohar* (loc. cit.) says that the 'divine name *ADaM* contains that which is above and below, thanks to its three letters, *A*(*lef*), *D*(*aleth*), and the final *M*(*em*)'.

The mystery of man is none other than the unity of all his states, which can be summarized in these three degrees: transcendent-divine, immanent-spiritual, and heavenly-earthly, or psychic-physical; these degrees form one single universal person who simultaneously synthesizes and 'explains' all-reality. The Edenic state of the first man implies full possession of uninterrupted consciousness, which links together these three aspects or fundamental degrees of his universal state. In this state, the human microcosm is in permanent and cognitive union with the macrocosm and the 'metacosm'; here man is the central being of creation, about whom all other celestial and terrestrial beings gravitate hierarchically and, in this state, he is likewise creation, in its synthetic totality, its prototypical form and its infinite essence.

5

In the beginning man was the whole universe and everything beyond it. In his pure transcendence he was the 'more-than-luminous darkness' and in his ontological or causal state he was the 'spiritual sun', every ray of which is a beatific and deifying emanation. In his immanent state, he was situated at first beyond the multitude of forms, beyond all individualization; he comprised all things in so far as they were spiritual archetypes, appearing not yet distinct but as one single light just like the myriad of solar rays on a cloudless day. He was one single omnipresent 'centre' in which *avir*, the 'very pure and imperceptible air', was hidden, before his act of substantial generation. It was only in emerging from this purely spiritual state, which is none other than that of prototypical creation – filled only with divine immanence and containing, in synthesis, the existential 'germs' of all things – that man appeared distinct and, with him, all creatures.

In his first distinguishable state, man was at the same time the most mysterious and the most evident of beings since he was manifested in all the worlds at the same time: while appearing on earth in his outer and Sefirothic form, he surpassed all other creatures in beauty, while his inner and ethereal 'body' filled and fed this whole world without distinction; his heavenly or subtle 'body' was as large as the whole of the heavens, of which he represented at one and the same time the 'centre', the 'measure' and the 'circumference': he crossed them like an 'axis', and each heaven was, as it were, a part of himself and revolved around his 'middle pillar' in accordance with a supra-spatial 'movement'

THE MYSTERY OF MAN

which was traced in its indefinite circumference. All heavenly and earthly creatures were nothing but his own aspects exteriorized in the form of his apparently 'separated' possibilities. The two worlds of 'separate' realities, the one subtle and the other corporal, were still full of grace. They were in their paradisal state, in which the rays of immanent man fully illuminated all created things and in which the vibrations of his love united every creature with its divine archetype. Existence, not only on the spiritual plane, but also on the subtle and corporeal levels, was entirely filled and inundated with the revelatory presence of God; and man, himself, before his 'fall', was this presence. Man, and all the creatures surrounding him and which he included synthetically in his universal totality, existed in their first purity, their perfect deiform state, their sanctity.

So long as the 'separate' did not run counter to the One, but through its deiform quality manifested the positive will of the Creator, the whole cosmos with its indefinite variations formed one beatific realm: the 'Kingdom of God', in which the One took pleasure in the multiple which he penetrated, illuminated and absorbed in love, and in which the multiple was immersed in the One in ecstasy and fusion with him. In this primordial realm, 'separation' from God led only to union with him. The dark void of the cosmos, manifested by the regulatory rigour of the Creator, was only the vessel open to the outpouring of his deifying grace. The difference between separation and union, emptiness and fullness, darkness and light, rigour and grace, world and God, was as though swept away by the unitive emanation of the universal principle, and existential conditions or limitations, as we know them and submit to them, in their dualistic and separative consequences through evil, suffering and death, could not yet be manifested. 'For (in the beginning) God did not create death, and he feels no joy from the loss of living creatures; he created all things for life (in him); the creatures of the world (in their first purity) are uncorrupted; they contain no principle of destruction (only a principle of transformation, whether of individualization or of universalization), and death has no dominion over the earth (in its primordial state) . . . For God created man for immortality and he made him in the image of his own nature. The envy of the devil (who opposes the unitive work of God) is the cause of the coming of death to the world; those who belong to him will experience it' (Wisdom of Solomon I, 13-14; II, 23-4).

In fact, so long as the created did not oppose union with the uncreated, the rigour inherent in the outer or cosmological state of separateness was not at all opposed to grace, immanent in the whole cosmos, but remained hidden in it. Only when Satan, the 'adversary' of the One, seduced man and caused him to commit the 'original sin' – forsaking uninterrupted union with God in favour of the 'forbidden fruit': dualism – were the antinomic powers of the cosmos let loose and the rigour of God emerged from his grace. The separative principle, rigour, began to act distinctly and in the opposite direction from grace, so as to deny everything which denied the One. Thus man, the universal mediator, brought about the complete reversal of the first cosmic order: the 'fall' of the created. What had formerly been one – even when there was apparent multiplicity – was separated; what had been raised up was brought down; what was hidden became manifest, and what was evident went into hiding; the inner became the outer, and the outer withdrew into the inner. The state of grace was superseded by the state of rigour; the cosmic blessing was changed into a curse: 'the soil shall be accursed because of thee'. The 'tree of life' – the divine and deifying spirit – of which man and all creatures could 'eat' to their liking, to appease their 'hunger' for the absolute, was hidden from their direct consciousness 'by the cherubim who, waving a flaming sword, guard the path of the Tree of Life'. 'Now, let him not advance his hand, nor take of the Tree of Life to eat of it and live eternally.' For man, in tasting the multiple, the composite, the ephemeral, has vowed himself, carrying all earthly creatures with him, to separation and death. 'The day on which thou shalt eat of it, thou shalt certainly die.' Ignoring this word of the One, but believing in that of Satan, his adversary, man broke his union with God and was divided in himself. His total being, which thus far had been but one with grace, the 'Tree of Life', joining everything to the most high, took on the appearance of distinctive rigour and, as regards earthly man, became like an axis broken up into innumerable existential levels which are separated from one another by a 'death'. Adam was no longer universal man who, synthetically, in one consciousness, united the divine-spiritual, subtle-psychic and gross-corporeal realities. At the moment when he began to feed on the 'tree of the knowledge of good and evil' his 'continuous' consciousness, penetrating and embracing all that is, was changed to a 'discontinuous' consciousness, whose spiritual-divine content only remained in him in a state of virtual knowledge, while the individual-human content, that is, the content of differentiating and fragmentary consciousness – and hence subject to error – took the whole place of actual knowledge. The intellection of paradisal and universal man, anchored in the unlimited vision of the One, was reduced to mental or discursive reflection and became attached to the sensory faculties, thereby obtaining simple perception and assimilation of earthly things. Until then, Adam, the integral manifestation of *metatron*, the cosmic intellect, and consequently of 'man above' was united with Eve – the perfect personification of *avir*, pure and universal substance – only in the *shekhinah*; in the midst of the cosmos they served as active or illuminating principle and receptive and generative principle, so that the whole of creation was ceaselessly reproduced through their divine union. Emerging from this spiritual union by forsaking divine immanence in favour of the 'knowledge of the one and the other', the pure and trans-lucid substantial nature of man was divested of its beatific and deifying light and 'left naked' in all its subtle and corporeal differentiations: 'The eyes of them both were opened, and they knew that they were naked', deprived of immanent unity. Thus, they caused the rigour which is inherent in substantial and dark nature to come out from spiritual grace which until then had kept it in itself as an aspect of creative mercy. 'And YHVH-*Elohim* sent him forth from the garden of Eden (from his first state) to till the ground (the substance) from whence he was taken (in his created nature).'

From then onwards created and substantial nature, dominated

by rigour, enveloped and confined grace, which had retired within itself and withdrawn to the inner depths of creation. The corporeal was no longer clothed in spiritual light which had become hidden inside the body in the innermost depths of the heart. The void left by grace, when it receded into the secret heart of creation – this void, which is none other than the fundamental cosmic manifestation of rigour – was filled by differentiated substance, nature, in all its existential evolution and gradation. This void, this deprivation of grace or presence of rigour, in its 'darkness' comprises evil, ignorance, error, scissions, oppositions, hatred: all dualistic emanations of Satan. These brought the separate realities, which exist in the inferior of the two formal worlds, into a desperate struggle in which one creature rose up against the other: 'Cain rose up against Abel his brother and slew him', and hid himself before his own divine essence, crying: "From thy face shall I be hid!" '

6

'YHVH saw that the wickedness of man was great in the earth, and that every inclination of the thoughts of his heart was only evil continually. And it repented YHVH that he had made man on the earth, and it grieved him at his heart. And YHVH said: I will blot out man whom I have created from the face of the earth; both man and beast, and creeping thing, and the fowl of the air; for it repenteth me that I have made them. But Noah found grace in the eyes of YHVH' (Genesis 6:5–8).

Why did Noah find grace in the eyes of the Eternal? Because he was 'in his generations a righteous and wholehearted man' because he 'walked with God' and through his deiformity attracted grace which was fleeing from the 'corrupted earth'. Because after the 'fall', grace, like the 'real presence' of God had remained amidst the weakening creatures like a redeeming light in the cosmic darkness, in order to soften through its merciful interventions the rigour of the universal Law which, for its part, regulates in perfect measure the ebb and flow of nature as well as the reactions proportionate to the actions of man. Indeed, grace is the spiritual and supernatural immanence of God in the midst of substantial and created nature, this immanence being in no way affected by existential vicissitudes, and constituting the necessary and immutable link between the transcendental cause and its cosmic effects. It dwells in the centre of the cosmos, in which is hidden the first state, the purely spiritual world of creation. This world being 'supernatural', is situated beyond the multiple, the composite or the corruptible, and, after as before the 'fall', is entirely filled with the manifest presence of God; it is the permanent 'state of grace', in the inmost depths of the subtle-psychical and gross-corporeal worlds.

Were it not for the gentle, vivifying and illuminating 'dew' which constantly falls from the 'tree' of grace into the two lower worlds where the multitude of creatures is unfolded, cosmic law in the rigour of its justice would at once destroy everything, 'from man even to cattle, to the reptiles and to the birds in the sky', because of the negation by man – the criterion of created existence – of his own reality, his pure 'self', which is God himself.

But this saving dew falls only inasmuch as there is a man on earth to attract it, for 'the whole earth', the entire cosmos, has been created only with a view to man, who is its synthesis and its mediator. If the natural movement of rigour is to descend into creation in order to dissolve it, and if the permanent tendency of grace is to flee from the 'prison' of nature and all created substance in order to return to its infinite transcendence, then the function of man is to cause grace to descend into the emptiness of cosmic 'deprivation', of earthly 'nothingness' filled with rigour, and to cause the latter, together with all created nature, to rise again into grace; his mission is to restore and to maintain the 'state of universal grace'.

When man acts rightly and 'walks with God', he attracts the manifestation of grace, which fills his inner emptiness and that of the whole world, and absorbs rigour into the divine light. But when man behaves badly and forsakes God, grace flees from him and from the whole of creation, making way for 'nothingness'.

By sinning, man attracts 'nothingness'; and rigour, in gainsaying the nothingness which could not exist in divine all-reality, annihilates man the sinner and his world; unless indeed grace intervenes in his favour, either as 'forgiveness' when he repents, or as 'long-suffering' when God grants him time to mend his ways. 'If thou doest well, (thy countenance) shall be lifted, and if thou doest not well, sin coucheth at the door, and unto thee is its desire, but thou mayest rule over it!' (Genesis 4:7).

'See, I have set before thee this day life and good, death and evil, in that I command thee this day to love YHVH, thy God, to walk in his ways, and to keep his commandments and his statutes and his ordinances; then thou shalt live. . . . But if thy heart turn away, and thou wilt not hear, but shalt be drawn away and worship other gods (idols or existential illusions) and serve them, I declare unto you this day that ye shall surely perish. . . . Choose life, that thou mayest live . . .' (Deuteronomy 30:15–19).

So long as man was nourished by the Tree of Life, by pure and unitive grace he was one with the One, and was in no way forced to choose between 'good', which contains eternal and divine life, and 'evil', which attracts rigour, destruction, death and damnation; he was forced to make this choice only from the moment when he forsook his union with God and actualized intellectual and existential dualism, the 'forbidden fruit'. From that time on, feeding on the 'tree of the knowledge of good and evil', man had to live the difference between union and separation, fullness and emptiness, light and darkness, grace and rigour, God and world; it was necessary that he suffer the 'nothingness' which separates and opposes all these aspects of the one and only reality, and that he seek his lost Paradise, his eternal good, in the return to the One, which is his beatific essence itself. For man to find again his universal and divine wholeness, immanent in the midst of 'fragments', he had to purify and spiritualize his body and his soul, by submitting them and making them accord with the supreme will and wisdom, and finally, by freeing himself from all his earthly bonds, from all his fragmentary or individual states. Henceforth, to be one with the One and again to become infinite in the infinite, a human being had to be separated from the separate and die to what is mortal, to what is finite.

Having actualized the reign of rigour, man had to take into consideration the 'commandments, laws and statutes' of the Lord, which are a negation of his negation of God. After breaking the marvellous vessel which the Creator had formed from the purest substance and filled to the brim with his own spirit – this cosmic vessel which was none other than universal man – the human individual had to gather and unite 'fragments', by the denial of evil and the affirmation of good, by permanent concentration of his whole being on the One, and to become again a sacred vessel ready, with God's forgiveness, to receive his illuminating and redemptive influx.

When God pardons, his rigour is reabsorbed into his clemency, and man passes from his state of sin, with all its dark consequences, to the state of grace which, in its entire fullness, reaches as far as spiritual illumination, the blissful and deifying vision of the One.

The return of man to his pure and divine essence is marked by these two principal 'stations': the 'primordial' or 'Edenic state' – which the Kabbalah calls *Shmittah* ('respite') – a state of perfect deiformity, implying the evident and permanent presence of God in man and the 'universal' or 'divine state', called *Yobel* ('Jubilee'), the state of supreme illumination and identity, of total union with God.[1] The pardon of God allows man to attain the first 'station', and the total influx of his light brings man to the 'goal'.

[1] These two principal 'stations' of spiritual liberation, that is, union with immanence and transcendence, are symbolically expressed, respectively, in the sacred institutions of the sabbatical year (*Shmittah*) and the Jubilee year (*Yobel*), both of which are opened by the sounding of the ritual horn, called the 'voice of the trumpet' (*kol shofar*), 'announcing every deliverance'. This is the 'voice' which came out of the divine 'trumpet' – as the 'primordial' and 'redeeming sound'—on Mount Sinai, when the people of Israel received from God the revelation of the Torah.

VII The Return to the One

I

The revealed tradition is the path which God had laid out for man so that he may find the way back to his first, theomorphic and essentially divine state: the way of the return to the One. Now, spiritual 'remoteness' from the divine origin is not the same for every human individual; it can even be said that it is different for every man according to the nature of his particular existential illusion, his attachment to the created 'otherness', which stands between him and divine 'selfness'. In its doctrinal formulations and dispensation of the 'means of grace', revelation takes into account the differences in 'relationships' between the human and the divine, differences in understanding and receptivity to the only reality. That is why traditional forms include many degrees of interpretation and application, a multitude of outer and inner, or exoteric and esoteric aspects.

Exotericism sees to the carrying out of the formal law, which leads to posthumous salvation, to a paradisaical and theomorphic existence of the human being; this is the way intended for the majority of believers, who are imprisoned in individualist or dualist illusion. From this point of view, the return to the One ends in the heavenly Paradise where the soul, freed from bodily fetters, contemplates the real presence of God. Because of the dualist point of view, which the majority of men do not succeed in surpassing during their earthly existence, exotericism describes this beatific vision as one of the 'delights' of 'nearness to God'; for esotericism, the same vision signifies spiritual knowledge which, whether directly or progressively, unites the knower with the known. In other words, the initiate knows that for the soul on which divine knowledge has been bestowed, 'nearness to God' is transformed into real identification with him and that it could not be otherwise, since in truth God is the 'One without a second'.

Esotericism, which expresses the 'unveiled' spirit hidden in the 'letter', is intended to lead a being, while still here on earth, beyond the symbolism of sacred forms and dualism of thought to this deifying knowledge; but it speaks only to those who, being moved by a spiritual receptivity of irresistible force – the 'thirst for the absolute' – seek truth through direct cognitive union with the only true One himself. For this minority – or 'elect' – paradise, or the primordial human state, is not only to be found beyond but also here below in the very 'heart' of man; it is his virtual state of union with God.

Exotericism – we are referring as always to the Jewish tradition – is the belief in one God, a belief which goes hand in hand with the affirmation of individual and 'extra-divine' existence, so that there is a dualism between the 'servant' and the 'Lord'. In esoteric or Kabbalistic tradition, this dualism is overcome by a monotheism which reaches its final conclusion, its real and infinite significance, where God is One, not only in his 'Lordship' but in his whole reality; he is the One in the absolute sense, the 'One without a second', the only reality, so that everything which exists is in essence God.

This conclusion from integral and orthodox monotheism should, however, not be taken for pantheism, in the philosophical and current meaning of the word; for, as has just been explained, the Kabbalah affirms the 'essential' identity of all things with the absolute, and not merely a 'co-substantiality' with it. The absolute, which is pure essence, contains the universal substance as the creative possibility, in the unlimitedness of its all-reality. Exotericism calls this possibility – the nature of which when all's said and done remains unintelligible – the 'nothingness', from which God brought forth the world; it speaks of a *creatio ex nihilo*, but the Kabbalah does not take this 'nothingness' literally, in view of the fact that God brings out something from it, so that it must necessarily contain something real.

In truth, this 'nothingness' is the receptivity or divine emptiness which, under the influence of *hokhmah*, 'wisdom', active cause, becomes passive, female or maternal cause, namely *binah*, creative 'intelligence'. Under the effect of the same influence, something of the emptiness of *binah* – this emptiness being actualized in *malkhuth*, the 'lower mother' or immediate cause of the cosmos – is 'contracted' and becomes created substance; therefore this substance is nothing but 'solidified' receptivity or emptiness. Now, since substantialization implies a becoming, substance has no permanence; it becomes concrete in the void and dissolves in it. When solidified, substance is like a dark mirror, receiving the luminous influx of divine wisdom, which is reflected in it, with everything manifestable and creatural which it radiates; when the substance dissolves and again becomes pure receptivity, these luminous and spiritual reflections are reabsorbed in the absolute essence. Thus, substance, while emanating from the only reality, is but vanity, illusion, arising and disappearing within reality like a fleeting shadow; it is that unintelligible possibility of the 'One without a second', which allows him, in the midst of himself, to take on the chimerical appearance of a 'second', of 'another than he', the mirage of a multiple world, creation. It is the antinomian or negative possibility of God which does not call itself God; of course, in itself, in its non-manifested and supreme state, it is divine receptivity, the passive cause itself, but in its manifested state, in which it is materialization, limitation, it is opposed to the infinite; it is opposed to it in order to affirm it by reflecting its light and by negating itself, by dissolving itself in the infinite.

Orthodox monotheism calls only the transcendent essence 'God' and calls his uncreated and immanent light his real presence; and it calls all pure spirits, all immortal souls, all manifestations which form the direct and illusorily 'multiplied' radiation of his immanence 'divine'. According to the pantheistic view, God is confused with the world, so that all created things are considered as divine, and even as God himself, in their ephemeral envelope; thus the distinction between good (spiritual, essential, real) and evil (attachment to the ego and the world—to 'vanity') is done away with. Now, the distinction between good and evil is the very basis of monotheistic law, while for the Kabbalist it becomes the discrimination between the real and the unreal, and this discrimination allows him to overcome existential illusion by the reintegration or dissolution of his substance in the inner emptiness, and the identification of his spirit with the fullness of essence.

The pantheist claims unreservedly that all is God, or that God is all. The monotheist says: in their uncreated state, all things are God; and in their created state, they manifest God more or less perfectly – down to dark 'counterfeits' – according to their degree of conformity or non-conformity with the divine. But all things equally contain God in the innermost part of themselves, although in their created state they move away from him or come closer to him in proportion to their deiformity or according as they represent more or less immediate 'envelops' of God; thus, the corporeal state envelops the psychic state, and the latter envelops the spiritual state which alone envelops God directly. Indeed, God is in everything, but manifested more or less perfectly, and 'veiled' differently by the existential degrees which are between him and such and such a thing. Finally, the Kabbalah affirms that everything is in God, whether in his cosmic presence, or in his transcendence; but it is only in his transcendence, in the absolute, that everything is he, and that he is everything, without any difference.

2

The Torah – the depository of Jewish monotheism, in both its exoteric and esoteric aspects – is summarized in the ten commandments which 'correspond to the ten *Sefiroth*'. Now, all the *Sefiroth* are identical with the One, of which they are the infinite and indivisible attributes; in the same way, the whole decalogue is reduced to the first commandment, the one which affirms the one God: 'I am YHVH your God, who has brought you out of the land of Egypt, out of the house of bondage; you shall have no other gods before my face' (Exodus 20:2). The confession of divine unity is thus the essential commandment of Judaism.[1]

[1] That it is why it is said that: 'He who professes idolatry repudiates the ten commandments' (*Sifre Numbers*, 111, 31b); 'The prohibition of idolatry is

In his 'Introduction to the duties of hearts', Bahya ibn Pakuda says on this subject: 'The unity of God is the principle and foundation of our religion. Through perfect confession of unity, faith is distinguished from unbelief. It is the real principle of our religion. He who turns away from it destroys his own works and his own faith. That is why the first words pronounced on Sinai were: "I am YHVH, thy Lord . . .; thou shalt have no other gods before my face." The call is still more urgent in the sentence: "Hear, O Israel, YHVH, our God, YHVH is one (*Shema Israel* YHVH *Elohenu* YHVH *Ehad*)" (Deuteronomy 6:4).[1] This phrase – which, because of its first word, is called the *Shema* – is the sacred confession of divine unity which a Jew is supposed to repeat at least twice a day, once in the morning and once in the evening.[2] Now,

---

equal in importance to all the other commandments of the Torah' (*Horayoth* 8a); and, 'Idolatry is so grave a matter that whoever rejects it acts as if he knew the Torah in its entirety' (*Hullin* 5a). Likewise in the Gospel, all the commandments of the Torah are summed up in the affirmation of the One, in himself and in the 'neighbour' or in his transcendence and immanence: 'Which is the first of all the commandments? Jesus answered: The first is: "Hear, O Israel, the Lord, our God, the Lord is One! And therefore thou shalt love the Lord, thy God, with all thy heart, with all thy soul, with all thy mind and with all thy strength." The second is this one: "Thou shalt love thy neighbour as thyself." There is no other commandment greater than these' (var. Matthew 22:40: 'These two commandments contain all the law and the prophets.') The scribe said unto him: 'Well, master, thou hast said the truth, for there is one God and there is none other than he; and to love him with all the heart, with all the understanding, and with all the strength, and to love his neighbour as himself is more than all whole burnt offerings and sacrifices.' (Mark 12:28–33)

[1] These two modes of the monotheistic profession of faith – the one negative, which excludes 'other gods', and the other positive, which affirms the only God – are to be found in Islam in the verses from the Koran: 'There is no divinity but Divinity.' (*La ilaha illa 'Llah*); and: 'Say: He is the one God (literally, the divinity).' (*Qul hua 'Llahu ahad.*)

[2] After Israel was forbidden to pronounce the name YHVH the name *Adonai*, 'My Lord', was substituted for it in the confession of faith in the *Shema*.

in the Scriptures, this confession is followed by the commandment: "And thou shalt love YHVH, thy God, with all thy heart,
with all thy soul, and with all thy might", regarding which the
Zohar says that he who confesses divine unity should do so "with
all his heart and with all his intelligence; all the limbs of his body
and all his organs should participate in this confession", which
thus becomes the concentration of the whole being on the One, a
concentration which could lead even to total absorption in the
only reality.' 'Happy is the portion of whoever can penetrate into
the mysteries of his (divine) Master and become absorbed into him,
as it were. Especially does a man achieve this when he offers up
his prayer to his Master in intense devotion, his will then becoming
as the flame inseparable from the coal (the spirit), and his mind
concentrated on the unity. . . . Whilst a man's mouth and lips are
moving, his heart (his spirit) and will must soar to the height of
heights (the supreme principle), so as to acknowledge (in truth)
the unity of the whole in virtue of the mystery of mysteries in
which all ideas, all wills, and all thoughts find their goal, to wit, the
mystery of the *en sof* (infinite, illimitable)' (*Zohar, Vayak'hel* 213b).

The confession of divine unity, which is the essential commandment of Jewish exotericism, thus becomes, in Kabbalistic
practice, the concentration of the whole man on the 'One without
a second', his union with God, which reverberates throughout the
universe. 'In all things there is a "drawing near" (to God) for him
who understands how to accomplish the union and to worship the
Lord, for when the (spiritual) sacrifice (of the ego and the world)
is offered in manner due, all (the existential and spiritual) grades
are brought near as one unity, and the light of the (divine)
countenance is present (in a state of revelation) in the world, in
the sanctuary (which means both the macrocosmic centre and the
heart of man), and the (satanic) "other side" is subdued and
covered in, and the side of holiness reigns in all as light and joy.
But when the sacrifice (of oneself and of all things) is not offered
in manner due (to the "One without a second"), and the union is
not effected, this (divine) countenance is overcast and the light is
not present, the moon (synonym of the *shekhinah*) is in hiding, and

the "other side" reigns, because there is no one who knows how to unify the holy name in the proper fashion' (*Zohar, Tetsaveh* 181b).

3

Affirmation of the One, to the point of union with him, is the essence of monotheism. 'Union' is called 'union of the name', when the divine name, invocation or prayer, are its operative support. The letters of the holy name – or the different names of God joined together in a certain manner in some ritual prayer – correspond to so many degrees or aspects of divine all-reality; 'to unite the name' is, through inner spiritual and universal realization, to unite all the worlds, large and small, of the only reality, all the possibilities of the One.

The union (of the fundamental aspects) of God is completely expressed in the three words: 'YHVH *Elohenu* YHVH'; that is why the *Shema*, which contains them, represents, for Israel, the central support for contemplating unity. Besides this, the name *Israel* is conjoined in it to the 'triple name' of God; and not to mention the word *ehad*, 'one', the word *Shema* itself, meaning 'listen', has great unitive power.

Bahya says: '*Shema* ("listen", "hear", "understand", "obey"), this term does not refer to hearing, to the fact of hearing with the ear, but to understanding, to the faith of the heart. . . .' According to the Kabbalah, the unitive power of the word *Shema* lies in the fact that it 'contains the seventy divine names', since it is composed of the word *shem*, 'name', and the letter *a (ayin)*, the numerical value of which is seventy. Therefore, *Shema*—like all the other words of the 'confession' – is itself a divine name, and its particular quality, or mode of manifesting the divine, is that it calls upon man to listen until his own cognitive faculty awakens. Man, when he pronounces the word *Shema* with concentration and with full knowledge of what he is about, actualizes in himself – with the help of God – the saving power of this name; his heart 'hears' the call of the One and is open to him.

The word *Shema* is both a word uttered by man and a divine name or power; likewise, the word *Israel* means both the man 'who struggles with God' and also 'holiness' or divine 'wisdom'. *Israel* is, therefore, the name of God which expresses not only his earthly manifestation in the form of the Chosen People but also the simultaneous revelation of his two aspects, 'sacred' and 'sapiential', which dominate the soul of this people. '*Rabbi* Jose said: "God first called Israel 'holy', (*kadosh*) as it is written, 'For thou art a holy (*kadosh*) people unto YHVH *thy God*" (Deuteronomy 14:2). Then he called them 'holiness' (*kodesh*), as it is written: 'Israel is the holiness (*kodesh*) of YHVH the first fruits of His increase' (Jeremiah 2:3). What is the difference between the two terms ('holy' and 'holiness')?"' '*Rabbi* Abba said: "Holiness is higher than all (which emanates from God, for it is called 'the first fruits of his increase', His first emanation: *hokhmah*, supreme 'wisdom'), for so we have learned that when all sanctities are combined, they are called 'holiness' and all (which has emanated and which is 'holy' in its pure essence) assemble together to that place (or divine state) which is called 'holiness' (or wisdom)."' '*Rabbi* Eliezar said: "The beginning and end of all is comprised in 'holiness', and the supreme wisdom (*hokhmah*, from which all emanates and to which all returns) is called 'holiness' . . . ' (*Zohar, Ha'aẓinu* 296b, 297a). After the soul, in the *Shema*, has been opened to God and to union with him, it has to realize its first, sacred and deiform state, Israel, the pure and empty 'mirror', which reflects no 'other gods', the existential illusions, but contemplates the only reality: YHVH–*Elohenu*–YHVH.

YHVH–*Elohenu*–YHVH. 'These three are one. How can the three names be one? Only through the perception of faith: in the vision of the Holy Spirit, in the beholding of the hidden eyes alone' (*Zohar, Bo* 43b). According to the various teachings of the *Zohar*, these three names represent the mystery of the 'summit of the rocks', the transcendent unity of the first causes or *Sefiroth*.

The first YHVH[1] is the triple 'head' or supreme cause, namely, *kether–hokhmah–binah*; it is the unity of the 'cause of causes', of 'active cause' and 'passive cause' or of the 'supreme crown', of

[1] Although the name YHVH is now pronounced *Adonai*, it is always written in its own form and its spiritual content is not changed.

'father' and 'mother'; in a broad sense, it is the whole of divine transcendence.

Elohenu (our God) is the 'root' or real 'source' of creation, the unity of the six active *Sefiroth* of cosmic 'construction': *hesed–din–tifereth–netsah–hod–yesod*; it is the 'son', of whom Scripture says (Isaiah 11:1): 'There shall come forth a shoot out of the stock of Jesse and a twig shall grow forth out of its roots.' The 'twig' which issues from the transcendent 'son' – the sixfold 'root' of all manifested things – is divine omnipresence; that is why *Elohenu* also means universal immanence or, in its saving aspect, universal redemption, the 'mystery of the future world'.

The final YHVH is the 'lower path', the last *Sefiroth*, *malkhuth*, the passive and direct cause of cosmic 'construction'; it is the 'daughter', or the 'lower mother' of creation, which descends like a 'path' right to this world below to create and penetrate all earthly things and carry them back to God. The last YHVH thus represents the immanence or real presence of God, in so far as it dwells and operates in our world, especially in Israel, in which it is the 'sacred community', the mystical body, with all the manifestations and means of grace that the latter comprises. Indeed, all the means of grace granted to the Jewish people are concentrated in the sacrosanct name YHVH, which contains, in a state of revelation, the fullness of the divine presence on earth.

When man contemplates the *Shema* in this way, in accordance with its spiritual content, and concentrates on it 'with all his heart, with all his soul, and with all his might', the *shekhinah* – so says the Kabbalah – descends into him and unites him with God; then, all aspects of reality, from the highest to the lowest, 'from the infinite to the end of creation', are united; the *Shema* has been transformed into a single word, a single name, a single reality: *ehad*, the 'One'.

VIII The Great Name of God

> *For from the rising of the sun,*
> *even unto the going down of the same,*
> *my name is great among the nations,*
> *and in every place offerings are presented*
> *unto my name.*

Malachi 1:11-12

1

The Judaic confession of divine unity, the scriptural formula of which – the *Shema* – combines several names of God, represents for the Jew one of the most important 'means of union'; another central or direct means of attaining union with God lies in the invocation of a single one of his names.

The tetragrammaton YHVH – the 'lost word' – was above all others the 'saving' name in the tradition of Israel; it is known as *shem hameforash*, the 'explicit name', the one, that is, of which every consonant reveals and symbolizes one of the four aspects or fundamental degrees of divine all-reality. It is also called the 'complete name' and the 'synthesis of syntheses', because it includes all the other divine names, each of which, by itself, expresses only one or another particular aspect of the universal principle; it is also called the 'unique name' because it is for the 'unique people', and more especially because of its incomparable spiritual efficacy, in that it gives the possibility of direct actualization of the divine presence (*shekhinah*). It was exactly on account of the direct outpouring of divine grace brought about by the invocation of the name YHVH that the traditional authority in Israel found it necessary, even before the destruction of the second Temple, to forbid the spiritually fallen people to invoke, or even merely to pronounce the tetragrammaton. In his 'Guide of the Perplexed', Maimonides says on this subject: 'A priestly blessing has been prescribed for us, in which the name of the Eternal (YHVH) is pronounced as it is written (and not in the form of a substituted name) and that name is the "explicit name". It was not generally known how the name had to be pronounced, nor how it was proper to vocalize the separate letters, nor whether any of the letters which could be doubled should in fact be doubled. Men who had received special instruction transmitted this one to another (that is, the manner of pronouncing this name) and taught it to none but their chosen disciples, once a week . . . There was also a name composed of twelve letters, which was holy to a lesser degree than the name of four letters; in my opinion it is most probable that this was not a single name but one composed of two or three names which, joined together, had twelve letters (representing their synthesis).[1] This was the name which was substituted for the name of four letters wherever the latter occurred in the reading (of the Torah), just as today we use the name beginning with the consonants *Alef, Daleth* (*A Do Na Y*, "My Lord"). Doubtless this twelve-letter name had originally a more special meaning than that conveyed by the name *Adonai*; it was not at all forbidden to teach it and no mystery was made of it in the case of any well-instructed person; on the contrary, it was taught to anyone who wished to learn it. This was not so in respect to the tetragrammaton; for those who knew it taught it only to their sons and disciples, once a week. However, as soon as undisciplined men, having learnt the twelve-letter name, began thereafter to profess erroneous beliefs – as always happens when an imperfect man is confronted by a thing which differs from his preconceived notion of it – they began to hide this name also and no longer taught it except to the most devout men of the priestly caste, for use when blessing the people in the sanctuary; it was indeed on account of the corruption of men that the pronunciation of the *shem hameforash* had already been abandoned, even in the sanctuary: "After the death of Simeon the Just", so say the Doctors, "his brother priests ceased to bless by the name (YHVH) but blessed

[1] Like the eight-letter name: YAHDVNHY, which is the synthesis of the two names YHVH and ADONAY (My Lord).

by the name of twelve letters". They also say: "At first it was transmitted to every man (in Israel), but after heedless men increased in number, it was no longer transmitted save to men of the priestly caste and the latter allowed (the sound) of it to be absorbed (during the priestly blessing) by the (liturgical) melodies intoned by their fellow-priests."'

Even after the destruction of the second Temple, however, invocation of the 'explicit name' appears to have continued as the sacred prerogative of a few initiates who were unknown to the outside world and who served as the spiritual poles of the esoteric 'chain of tradition' (*shalsheleth hakabbalah*). The function of this chain is the initiatic transmission – uninterrupted through the ages – of the 'mysteries of the Torah', which include, among others, the mystery of the invocation of the holy names; except for the extremely restricted 'elect' who retain the high function of guarding and secretly invoking the 'complete name',[1] no one may know its exact pronunciation. Although today Hebrew scholars render the name YHVH by 'Jehovah' on the strength of the Masoretic vocalization given in the Bibles and prayerbooks, or by 'Yahveh', in an attempt to imagine some way to pronounce it, these introductions of vowels into the tetragrammaton certainly do not correspond to the authentic pronunciation, and that is why it is written here only in the form of the four consonants which are its known basis.

The prevailing ignorance as regards the pronunciation of the 'explicit name' is certainly not the result of mere 'forgetfulness' nor of a purely human decision arrived more than two thousand years ago. The suppression of the teaching and pronunciation of this name – by decree of the traditional authority – is so categorical and so radical in its consequences that it can be affirmed that God himself has withdrawn this name from the mass of the people

[1] According to the word of God addressed to Moses: 'Thou shalt say unto the children of Israel: "YHVH, the God of your fathers, the God of Abraham, the God of Isaac and the God of Jacob hath sent me to you. This is my name for ever, and this is my memorial (*zikhri*, the invocation of God) unto all generations"' (Exodus 3:15).

of Israel. However, such intervention 'from above' expresses not only the rigour, but also the mercy of God, who foresaw that the human recipients of 'the last days', no longer possessing the requisite theomorphism, would be shattered by the weight of his lightning descent.

The 'complete name', therefore, cannot be the medium for deifying invocation in our age, which in the prophecies is called the 'end of time'; this being so, we must consider its fragmentary substitutes without particular reference to the 'twelve-letter name', the ritual use of which lasted only a short time. As we have seen, it had to be replaced by the name *Adonai*, which has been pronounced, ever since the destruction of the Temple, every time the tetragrammaton occurs in the reading of the Torah and the daily prayers. It should be noted that the substitution of the name *Adonai* was decreed only in respect to the exoteric ritual, whether performed in the synagogue or in private, the aim of which is the salvation of the soul in a restricted sense, that is, within the confines of the ego; it does not have in view the invocation which is intended to raise man's being to the highest 'place' (*hamakom*) which embraces all that is. The restriction does not apply to the 'two-letter name', YH (יה), which is pronounced *Yah* (יה) and is nothing other than the first half of the 'name of four letters', YHVH (יהוה); from the very fact that it is directly substituted for the *shem hameforash*, this name must have the same esoteric potentialities as the latter, without, however, involving the danger of a too sudden actualization of the divine.[1] This even appears obvious, firstly because the 'name of two letters' has the same transcendent significance as the tetragrammaton, which includes it and further, in a more general way, because every divine name

[1] In his commentary on the *Sefer Yetsirah* written in 931, Gaon Saadya de Fayyum says: 'When it is said: "YaH has two letters, YHVH has four letters", what is meant is that YaH is one half of the name YHVH. Now, the half was said everywhere and at all times, but the whole was only said in the Sanctuary in a particular period and at the moment of the blessing of Israel.' And the Talmud (*Erubin* 18b) states: 'Since the destruction of the Sanctuary, the world need only use two letters (as a means of invocation, that is, the two first letters of YHVH, forming the name YaH).'

not referring to a particular quality to the exclusion of other qualities, refers to the being or essence of God.

2

In order fully to grasp the spiritual significance of the name *Yah*, we have to return once more to the metaphysical basis of the name YHVH, of which it forms an integral part. Now comprehension of the foundation of the holy names, as they were revealed to the Jewish people, is connected with the comprehension of the ten *Sefiroth* which themselves represent the 'contemplative names' of God. Each *Sefirah*, although synthetically invoked through one of the letters of YHVH, has besides an 'appellative name' of its own.[1] As we have already pointed out, *ehyeh*, 'being', is the name proper to *kether*, while *Yah* refers to *hokhmah*, the first and undifferentiated emanation of being; *Yehovih* – YHVH vocalized as *elohim*, 'gods', is the name of *binah*, for through it the all-reality, YHVH, begins to be revealed in distinct emanations or 'Gods'; *El*, 'God', or *Elohai*, 'my God', signifies the personal God, or the *Sefirah hesed*, divine 'grace'; *Elohim*, 'Gods' – the One in distinctive or separative manifestation – is the name of *din*, 'judgement' or universal discrimination; YHVH designates *tifereth*, 'beauty', or *da'ath*, 'omniscience', the whole consciousness of God, uniting his transcendent aspects (the ideogram of which is YH) with his immanent aspects (symbolized by VH);[2] YHVH *Tsebaoth*, 'YHVH of the Hosts', designates the principle of the affirmative cosmic powers, *netsah*, divine 'victory'; *Elohim Tsebaoth*, 'Gods of the Hosts', is the appellative name of the principle of the negative cosmic powers, *hod*, divine 'glory'; *El hai*, the 'living God', or *Shaddai*, the 'all-powerful', is a synonym of *yesod*, cosmic 'foundation', the eternal, creative and redemptive act of the *Sefiroth*;

---

[1] In certain Kabbalistic schools, the proper names of the *Sefiroth* themselves were used as 'appellative names'.

[2] Besides being applied particularly to *tifereth*, the tetragrammaton is the 'universal name' par excellence, the name which includes all names, all *Sefiroth*.

and *Adonai*, 'my Lord', signifies the immediate and 'maternal' cause of the cosmos, *malkhuth*, the 'kingdom' of God.

Before explaining in a more precise way the spiritual content of the names Y H V H and *Yah* by means of their Sefirothic synonyms, we should consider for a moment the outer forms of these names, which has a special and very great significance, particularly from the operative point of view. In their form, which is abstract and non-comparative, these two names are indeed different from a name such as *Adonai*; their content on the plane of ideas is not to be found, as in *Adonai*, in a direct analogy with some notion derived from the created and, more particularly, from human qualities and activities, but above all in the symbolism of the consonants and of their vocalization and punctuation (so far as these are known). One knows that the letters of the Hebrew alphabet and the way to pronounce them in order to form one word or another are a part of the mystery of sacred language, in which every consonant and every vowel, as well as every punctuation mark, indicates the eternal archetypes or divine aspects. The 'science of letters', which, thanks to the fact that every Hebrew consonant represents a definite number, is linked with the 'science of numbers', gives cognitive and operative access to these mysteries; but what is important for us here is simply to show the origin of the sacred 'ideography' or 'ideophony' which creates names such as Y H V H and *Yah* and is to be distinguished from the formation of names by analogy or comparison. Whereas comparison in regard to God has chiefly to do with his existential aspects – his relationships with the cosmos – the abstract and ideophonic names refer to his essential and integral aspects, as for instance, *Yah* to transcendence, and Y H V H to his all-reality. Ideophony makes it possible to synthesize the most diverse attributes in one short and harmonious name, as in the tetragrammaton, and also to express the highest ontological realities, bordering on the ineffable, as in the case of *Yah*; thus he who practices invocation is given the possibility, on the one hand, of directly integrating all the apparent antinomies of the divine into the unity of the one reality, and on the other hand, of going beyond every comparison or cosmic 'image' of the divine, that is, of becoming absorbed in that which is without form, without limit, without any definition whatsoever. We do not mean to say that comparative names like *Adonai* are lacking in sacred ideophony; yet their operative significance lies primarily in their literal and analogical meaning and only secondarily in their ideographic and numerical meaning, whereas the abstract names are *a priori* beyond literal and comparative meaning, from which they are liberated like 'kernels' from the 'nutshell', in such a way that they cannot be perfectly understood discursively (even if their implied meaning of 'to be' is known, as it happens for YHVH and *Yah*) without the help of the Sefirothic symbolism of their letters.

Thus the letter *yod* (Y = י), in YHVH and *Yah*, is revealed on the discursive level as the sacred ideogram of the undifferentiated unity of the ten *Sefiroth* – for the *yod* has the numerical value of ten – and in particular of the unity of the two supreme *Sefiroth*: *kether*, the 'crown', and *hokhmah*, 'widsom'. The fine upper point or 'crown' of the י designates *kether*; it is the supreme 'root', the root of being (*ehyeh*) in the midst of super-being (*ain*), itself 'symbolized' by empty space, the absence of any symbol. From this infinitesimal point, lost in the superintelligible, springs the first cognitive and active emanation, *hokhmah* – the 'father' – shown by the thick, horizontal stroke of the י and ending in a fine descending line which symbolizes being as it turns towards its manifestation.

The second letter of YHVH and *YaH*, the *he* (H = ה), is called the supreme 'mother', synonym of *binah*, the ontocosmological 'intelligence' of God, or his receptivity, which is the passive cause. This is the second emanation of *kether*, the third *Sefirah*, which, together with the first two, constitutes the name *YaH*, the 'transcendent half' of YHVH.

According to the *Zohar*, the union of the *yod* (the 'father' or active principle, *hokhmah*) with the *he* (the 'mother' or passive cause, *binah*) produces the *vav* (V = ו), called the 'son'. The letter *vav* has the numerical value of six, and in fact represents the metaphysical synthesis of the six active *Sefiroth* of cosmic construction': *hesed, din, tifereth, netsah, hod* and *yesod*. The *vav*, or 'son', is also called *da'ath*, universal 'knowledge', omniscience or consciousness of all God's ontological emanations and cosmic manifestations, which 'transmits the (Sefirothic) heritage to the daughter'.

The 'daughter' is the last *he* of the name YHVH, the symbol of the *Sefirah malkhuth*, 'kingdom'; this is the last of the seven *Sefiroth* of cosmic 'construction', namely, their passive aspect; in other words, it is the receptive cosmological principle, the un-created and creative substance, fed by the 'son' or active mediator, from which it receives all the Sefirothic emanations and projects them onto the cosmic plane.

This is how the divine 'family' is constituted, identical with the 'complete name': the 'father' (Y), the 'mother' (H), the 'son' (V) and the 'daughter' (H), the last being inseparable from the *vav* or universal spirit, which would not be able to manifest its dazzling irradiation on the cosmic plane, without the covering, simul-taneously protective and generative, of 'pure and imperceptible substance'.

As we have just seen, there is a parallelism between the two first and the two last letters of the tetragrammaton, its 'transcen-dent half' YH being reflected in its 'immanent half', VH. The *yod*, or active ontological principle, manifests in creation through *vav*, the active cosmological principle, which, from the ideographic point of view, appears in fact as the prolongation downward, or a 'descent' (ו) of the 'supreme point' (י). Similarly, the two *he* of the *shem hameforash* express the one maternal and receptive principle, seen first in its ontological aspect and then in its cosmic function. *Binah*, therefore, is called the '*upper he*', or the 'supreme mother', and *malkhuth* is called the 'lower *he*', the 'lower mother' or the 'daughter'. Let it be added that the letter *he* has the numerical value of five, so that the two *he* together, *binah* and *malkhuth*, make the number ten; they are the two divine 'coverings' which, in the passive mode, contain the entire Sefirothic decade.

Finally, and still in relation to the same symbolism, the four letters of the name YHVH signify in particular the archetypes of the 'four worlds' or fundamental degrees of divine all-reality. The *yod* (*kether-hokhmah*) represents the archetype of *olam ha'atsiluth*, the ontological 'world of emanation', which is nothing other than the infinite level of the ten *Sefiroth*. The first *he* (*binah*) symbolizes the archetype of *olam haberiyah*, the ideal 'world of creation', a purely spiritual level on which dwells the divine immanence (*shekhinah*). The *vav* (the unity of the six active Sefiroth of cosmic 'construction') is the archetype of *olam hayetsirah*, the subtle, celestial and psychic 'world of formation', the cosmic level on which dwell angels, souls and genii, on various planes. The final *he* (*malkhuth*), is the archetype of *olam ha'asiyah*, the sensory 'world of fact', the corporeal universe.

3

Since the 'complete name' was withdrawn from the Jewish people, they have used above all the following three names, which together replace the unity of the 'four letters'; firstly the name *YaH* which integrates the two first letters – the 'transcendental half' – of YHVH; secondly the name *Elohenu*, 'Our God', which includes the six active causes of cosmic construction and represents divine immanence as first revealed in the subtle, celestial and psychic world, symbolized by the *vav*; thirdly the name *Adonai*—an exoteric replacement for the name YHVH—designates *malkhuth*, the final *he*, representing divine immanence as manifested particularly in the corporeal world.

But the name which concerns us here is *Yah*, the transcendental nature of which leads, in principle, to the state of *Yobel* (Jubilee), final 'deliverance' (in the same sense as the Hindus understand the word *moksha*). This name seems to represent not only the 'means of grace' *par excellence* of the final cycle of Jewish history, but also that of its beginning. In fact, it can be deduced from Scripture that *Yah* was the divine name used particularly by Jacob and his people, whereas YHVH was the 'name of Israel' so long as Israel represented the 'portion of YHVH'. In the Psalms

(135:3-4) it is said: 'Praise *Yah*, for he is good! YHVH, sing praises to his name, for it is pleasant! For *Yah* has chosen Jacob unto himself, and Israel for his costly possession', the possession, that is, of YHVH, according to Deut. (32:9) 'For the portion of YHVH is his people'. And Isaiah (44:5) explicitly distinguishes between the 'name of Jacob' and the 'name of Israel': 'One shall call himself by the name of Jacob (*Yah*) and another shall subscribe with his hand, unto YHVH and surname himself by the name of Israel.' This distinction can be explained in relation to the history of Israel, all the phases of which are contained in three fundamental cycles: the first, or 'patriarchal' cycle, from Shem to Jacob's victorious struggle at Peniel with the divine manifestation; the second, or 'Israelite', cycle, from Peniel, where Jacob and his people received the name of Israel, to the destruction of the second Temple; and the third, or 'final', cycle, from the collapse of the priestly service and theocracy to the advent of the Messiah. Now Shem was the 'seed' of the Jewish race; Abraham was the 'father of many peoples' and Isaac the 'sacrifice of oneself to God', while Jacob gave birth to the twelve tribes and the 'mystical body' of Israel; so the latter is considered above all others as the patriarch of Israel and the people of God are called 'Jacob' until the struggle at Peniel.

'Jacob was chosen to belong to *Yah*', that is, to be raised up in spirit to divine transcendence. But at Peniel there was a fundamental change in the mystical destiny of Jacob and his people, for it was said to him (Genesis 32:28): 'Thy name shall be called no more Jacob, but Israel (he who struggles with God), for thou hast striven with God and with men and hast prevailed.' In the language of the Kabbalah this means that after having 'wrestled with God until victory' – absorption in the transcendence of *Yah* – Jacob prevailed also at Peniel over the divine manifestation called 'man', that is, over the 'descent' of God into humanity. This revelatory and redemptive 'descent' is symbolized, in sacred ideography, by the *vav* (ו). According to the *Zohar* (*Terumah* 127a): 'When the *vav* emerges mysteriously self-contained from the *yod-he* (*YaH*), then Israel attains to his costly possession', its *corpus mysticum*, which is identical with the *Sefirah malkhuth*, represented by the last *he* of the tetragrammaton. Thus, thanks to the sacred struggle of its patriarch, the people entered into possession of the reality hidden in the last two letters of the *shem hameforash* – the spiritual (V) and substantial (H) fullness of the divine immanence – and itself became, in its mystical body, the 'final *He*', the 'portion of YHVH'.

It appears, therefore, that during the 'Jacobite' phase the people were not yet the 'possession of YHVH', just as YHVH, – the 'complete name' or actualized unity of divine transcendence (YH) and divine immanence (VH) – was not yet the 'possession of Israel'. The people of 'Jacob' was centred on the transcendent aspect of God: *Yah*. In that cyclical moment and in that environment, spiritual realization must not necessarily have required initiation into the sacred sciences (symbolized by the *vav*), any more than it needed the priestly service in the sanctuary (represented by the last *he* of the tetragrammaton). It was only when YHVH established the roots of the earthly centre of his presence in the midst of Jacob's family – which thereby became 'Israel', or the Chosen People – that the *vav* or 'mysteries of the faith' had to be communicated to it through the intermediary of its patriarch. These mysteries, transmitted from generation to generation to the 'children of Israel', were lost at the time of their servitude in Egypt, but were reborn and permanently crystallized in the revelation on Sinai; and the 'final *he*' of YHVH, the pure and imperceptible substance of the *shekhinah*, called the 'Community of Israel', entered into the Holy Land and took up its abode in the Temple of Jerusalem, where the High Priest blessed all the people by the *shem hameforash*.

By the grace of the 'complete name', the Chosen People long ago actualized the 'kingdom of God' in the Holy Land, but on account of their sins the first Temple was destroyed and Israel had to suffer exile in Babylon. ' . . . during the whole seventy years of exile', says the *Zohar* (*Shemoth* 9b), 'Israel had no divine light to guide her and, truly, that was the essence of the exile. When, however, Babylon's power was taken away from her and Israel returned to the Holy Land, a light did shine for her, but it was not as bright as before (when Israel received the emanation of the "complete name", which was broken up by the sins which also caused the destruction of the first Temple), being only the emanation of the "lower *he*" (the *shekhinah*, or "mystical body" of Israel, identical with that of the second Temple), since the whole of Israel did not return to purity to be a "peculiar people" as before. Therefore, the emanation of the supernal *yod* did not descend to illumine in the same measure as before, but only a little. Hence Israel was involved in many wars until "the darkness covered the earth" and the "lower *he*" was darkened and fell to the ground (so that Israel was forbidden to invoke the "complete name") and the upper source was removed as before (as at the time of the destruction of the first Temple), and the second Temple was destroyed and all its twelve tribes went into exile in the kingdom of Edom.[1] The *he* also went into exile there . . . ' the *shekhinah* was 'decentralized', dispersed with Israel all over the world. It continued to radiate only through weak 'reflections' wherever there was a community of orthodox Jews; nevertheless, its sacred 'embers' have continued to flare up with an increased light and, sporadically, its true 'grandeur' has been recaptured amidst the elect; these are the *Mekubbalim*, or initiated Kabbalists, who – with certain exceptions, such as the 'false Messiahs' – formed the 'pillars' of the exiled people; but they appear to have become a negligible minority in the era of the triumph of 'Edomite' civilization, this modern world of ours which has even been transplanted to the Holy Land itself.

[1] The name of the biblical kingdom of Edom (situated between the Dead Sea and the Gulf of Elath) is here used as a symbolic term of the whole Roman Empire. According to the Kabbalah, Edom symbolizes sometimes the imperfect or unbalanced state of creation preceding its present state – the latter being an ordered manifestation of the *Fiat Lux* – and sometimes the idolatrous world of antiquity and, by extension, every materialistic, profane, or atheistic civilization, such as our own. The Bible (Genesis 36) identifies Edom with Esau, who sold his birthright – implying the right of the first-born, the major patriarchal blessing – for 'a mess of pottage'. Therefore, in the Jewish tradition, Esau or Edom is opposed to Jacob or Israel, as the animal and materialistic tendency of man is opposed to his spiritual and theomorphic tendency.

According to the *Zohar*, David, through the holy spirit, foresaw the end of the last exile of Israel – identifying it with the very 'end of days' in accordance with the prophecies – and revealed it in Psalm 102:19:[1] 'This shall be written for the future (or the last) generation and a people which shall be created (in the time of the "end") shall praise *Yah*!' The same prophecy is hidden in the verse from Malachi (3:23): 'Behold, I will send you Elijah (my God is *Yah*) the prophet (whose very name reveals which divine name was to be invoked during his pre-Messianic ministry and who represents, not only the type of the eternal master of masters, but also the type of all prophetic activity preceding and directly preparing the universal redemptive act of God's annointed), before the coming of the great and terrible day of YHVH.' Finally, the *Zohar* shows the exact reason why the name *Yah* – as in the time of Jacob – represents the means above all others of salvation in the period from the destruction of the Temple to the advent of the Messiah; and this reason becomes fully apparent in our day, when even the believing Jews can no longer live in freedom from the materialistic and profane organization of the modern world and so are unable any longer perfectly to carry out the Mosaic law, which presupposes as its 'sphere of activity' either a theocracy or a closed traditional world.[2] Now, the *Zohar* (*Terumah* 165b) says, referring to the name *Yah*: 'All is included in this name: those that are above (epitomized in the *yod*, the ideogram of pure transcendence, *kether-hokhmah*) and those that are below (hidden, in its

---

[1] This Psalm is called the 'prayer of the unhappy man' whose 'days vanish into smoke' and 'are like a shadow at its decline'. These phrases refer to the end of time.

[2] That the 'name of two letters' applies to the present time is made clear not only in the saying from the Talmud (*Erubin* 18b) which we have quoted, but also in the following formulation, amongst others, which was used in the school founded by the great master Isaac Luria (1534-72) and which shows that a spiritual method was based upon it as modern times approached: 'For the sake of union of the Holy One, be he blessed, with his *shekhinah*, in fear and in love, that the name *Y"H*, be blessed, may be unified in complete unification.' It should be remembered that the phrase 'to unify the name' has the meaning, from the point of view of method: to invoke the divine name.

THE UNIVERSAL MEANING OF THE KABBALAH

principial and undifferentiated state, in the "upper *he*", *binah*, the archetype of immanence). In it the six hundred and thirteen commandments of the Torah, which are the essence of the supernal and terrestrial mysteries, are included.' When this name is invoked sincerely, then it is as though one were carrying out all the commandments of the Jewish religion. This name compassionately forgives and compensates for the inadequacy of man in relation to the divine will; that is why the psalmist and 'prophet of *Yah*' cried out: 'In my anguish I called upon *Yah*; *Yah* heard my prayer and set me in a large place' (Psalm 118:5). 'I shall not die, I shall live and declare the works of *Yah*. *Yah* has chastened me sorely, but he has not given me over to death. Open the gates of righteousness before me; I will enter into them, praising *Yah*!' (Psalms 118:17–19). God can and will save Zion, not by his rigour, but by his compassion, when 'time shall have come to its end': 'Thou wilt arise and have compassion upon Zion; for it is time to be gracious unto her, for the appointed time is come!' (Psalms 102:13).[1]

4

The name *Yah* does not have the 'descending' efficacy of the *shem hameforash*; it lacks the direct influx of the *vav* or 'living God', the spiritual brilliance of which cannot be borne without the presence of the 'final *he*', represented at the same time by the

[1] 'For He hath looked down from the height of his sanctuary; from heaven did YHVH behold the earth to hear the groaning of the prisoner (of the civilization of "Edom") and to loose those that are appointed to death (represented by the anti-spiritual life of the modern world)' (Psalms 102:19–20). 'YHVH is full of compassion and gracious, slow to anger and plenteous in mercy. He will not always contend, neither will he keep his anger forever. He hath not dealt with us after our sins, nor requited us according to our iniquities, for as the heaven is high above the earth, so great in his goodness towards them that fear him. As far as the east is from the west, so far hath he removed us from our transgressions. Like a father hath compassion upon his children (and *Yah* is precisely the name of the divine "father", *hokhmah*) so hath YHVH compassion upon them that fear him. For he knoweth our frame; He remembereth that we are dust (and can in no way change the cyclical conditions in which we are born and have to live)' (Psalms 103:8–14).

THE GREAT NAME OF GOD

Temple and its priestly service, the transmission and practice of
the sacred sciences, the functioning of theocratic institutions, and
the conformity of an entire people to the divine will. Yet the
reasons for the substitution of the name *Yah* for that of YHVH are
not only restrictive, for, since they are connected, from the cyclical point of view, with the 'end of time', this end ceases also to be
of a purely negative character; on the contrary, according to the
prophets, it preceeds a positive renewal, namely, the creation of 'a
new Heaven and a new earth' – more perfect than those now
existing – as well as the creation of a new Jerusalem, whose 'places
shall be sacred to YHVH and will never be laid waste nor destroyed'. By the very fact that it is the name to be invoked by the
'last generation', *Yah* is also the name for the return to the 'beginning', to the perfect original of all things. It is different from the
tetragrammaton, the efficacity of which is above all 'descending',
revelatory and existential, for the name *Yah* is in fact the name of
'ascent' and of redemption; it is exactly the name of the 'beginning' and of the 'end' of every ontological emanation and cosmic
manifestation of God, while the name YHVH is the whole emanation, and the whole manifestation.

The 'upper (or transcendant) YHVH' manifests through the
'lower (or immanent)[1] YHVH'; in the same way, the 'upper (or
ontological) *Yah*' manifests through the 'lower Yah' or cosmic
principle, which retains its transcendent nature everywhere, even
'below'. Therefore, if the 'lower YHVH' represents divine immanence, the 'lower *Yah*' then represents 'transcendent immanence'.
The *yod* which, in its pure transcendence 'on high' is the unity of
kether and *hokhmah*, signifies 'below', in the metacosmic centre of
the cosmos, the unity of the *shekhinah* and its active aspect, *metatron*, the cosmic intellect, the inner regulator of creation, while the
following *He* represents its passive aspect *avir*, 'ether', the quintessence – the *He* having in fact the numerical value of five – of the

[1] These two aspects of YHVH are revealed to Moses in the Scriptures
(Exodus 34:6) when God shows him His attributes (*Middoth*) beginning with
the twice repeated: 'YHVH YHVH *El rahum wehanun* . . . ' (YHVH YHVH,
God merciful and compassionate . . .).

four subtle and the four coarse elements; it is, as we have already seen, the undifferentiated principle of all subtle, celestial or psychic substance and of all coarse or corporeal matter. If the *shekhinah*, in so far as it dwells in the prototypical and spiritual world (*olam haberiyah*), is the 'transcendent immanence' of *kether*, then *metatron* is that of *hokhmah* and *avir* that of *binah*; now just as the three highest *sefiroth* cannot be separated one from another, since they represent the one infinite and indivisible principle, *Yah*, so also *metatron* and *avir* must not be separated from the *shekhinah*, of which they are respectively the active or regulating aspect and the receptive or generative aspect. These three immanent principles, undifferentiated, compose the 'lower *Yah*', also called the 'heaven of heavens', the inseparable unity of the tenth, ninth and eighth heaven being 'the one who rides in *Araboth*,[1] (the seventh heaven): *Yah* is his name (Psalms 68:5). The 'heaven of heavens', identical with the prototypical 'world of creation' (*olam haberiyah*) is the intermediary plane between the Sefirothic 'meta-cosmos' and the created cosmos which begins in the seventh heaven, *Araboth*, the 'surface of the lower waters'. The 'lower *Yah*' is therefore 'transcendent immanence', the mediator between pure transcendence and immanence in that it penetrates that which is created and is called by the last two letters of the 'lower YHVH'.[2]

[1] It should be remembered that the word *Araboth* for the Seventh heaven, translated sometimes as 'clouds', sometimes by 'plains', 'desert' or 'heaven', is derived from the root ARB, which means something mixed. In fact, *avir*, the undifferentiated ether, that 'pure and imperceptible air' of the eighth heaven, is manifested in *Araboth* in its first differentiation, subtle substance or 'water' which reflects the uncreated light, or spiritual 'fire' descending from the *shekhinah* or from its universal irradiation, *metatron*. Now the 'surface of the waters' shines so brightly in the light of the divine 'fire' that it seems to be utterly fused or 'mixed' in it. This 'mixture' or more precisely this 'immanence' of the spirit in the subtle substance, which endures as long as the cosmos subsists, produces the whole of the seven 'heavens', *shamaim*, this word being composed of *esh*, spiritual 'fire' and of *maim*, substantial 'waters'.

[2] The *vav* of the 'lower YHVH – having the numerical value of six – symbolizes the *shekhinah* which penetrates the first six of the seven heavens constituting the subtle 'world of formation' (*olam hayetsirah*). The 'final *he*' of the 'lower YHVH' – having the numerical value of five – represents *avir*, the quint-

When YHVH comes down from the highest 'place' to the centre of this world, he brings the secrets of all the divine and cosmic degrees, the 'mysteries of the Torah' with their various graces; thus his 'four letters' form what is pre-eminently the revealing name, while *Yah* is enthroned on the 'surface of the waters', where the 'heavens and the earth' begin and end, that is to say the whole of the world 'created in one single instant'; there it is that all creatures emerge from God and return to him, in a single 'cry of joy' which is nothing other than the 'primordial sound'. The name *Yah* is the revealed utterance of this inarticulate and universal 'cry' or 'sound' which manifests and reabsorbs the entire cosmos; it is the name of creative and redemptive joy. Thus the Psalmist cries out: 'Make way for him who rides in *Araboth*: *Yah* is his name. Rejoice before him!' 'What the verse tells us', comments the *Zohar* (*Terumah* 165b), 'is that the ancient of ancients (the supreme principle) rideth in the *Araboth* (that he is really present) in the sphere of *Yah*, which is the primordial mystery emanating from him, namely the ineffable name *Yah*, which is not identical with him (the absolute), but is a kind of veil emanating from him. This veil is his name, it is his chariot, and even that is not manifested (in the cosmos, but is enthroned on the "surface of the waters"). It is his "great name". . . . For when all is well with this name, then harmony is complete, and all worlds rejoice in unison.'

Yah, in its immanent aspect, is the immediate cause of the cosmos, the cause that transcends all its effects: it remains hidden in the prototypical world, as uncreated and infinite light. But its irradiation transpierces its envelope, the ether, with a 'sound' which is that of the revelatory, creative and redemptive 'word'; this is the 'voice' of the Creator, the 'primordial sound' which produces the two lower worlds, the world of subtle 'formation'

---

essence, in that it has descended into the lowest heaven, there to dwell as the ether or undifferentiated principle of the four elements constituting *olam haasiyah*, the sensory or corporeal 'world of fact'; thus the 'final *he*', dwelling in the lowest heaven, is the immediate and omnipresent centre of our world.

and the sensory world of 'fact'. It is the 'inner voice' which sounds in the innermost depths of all things, so that it is said that 'the heavens declare the glory of God, and the firmament showeth his handiwork. Day unto day uttereth speech and night unto night revealeth knowledge. There is no speech, no language where the sound is not heard: their voice resounds through all the earth and their words go out to the end of the world . . . '(Psalms 19:2–5).

5

The 'inner' (divine) voice' is in truth the very light of God, an infinite light which, by refraction in the ether, has been transformed into revelatory, creative and redemptive 'sound'. That is the universal 'name' of God, inwardly his light, outwardly his voice, emitted spontaneously and in innumerable modes – articulate or inarticulate – by 'everything that has a soul'. This is why the Psalmist calls, not only to men, but to everything he sees as animated by the universal name, to invoke that name for the glory of the 'named' and the salvation of the world; he even goes so far as to exhort the 'heaven of heavens' to join in the invocation, because it is from there, from *Yah* itself, that the voice in effect descends and resounds on the 'surface of the waters' – where the created heavens begin – and is thence transmitted throughout the whole of existence, even to the earthly 'abysses'. 'Praise *Yah*! Praise YHVH from the height of the heavens! Praise him in the heights! Praise ye him, all his angels! All his hosts, praise ye him! Praise ye him, sun and moon! Praise him, all ye stars of light! Praise him, ye heavens of heavens and the waters that are above the heavens! . . . Praise YHVH from below on the earth, ye sea-monsters and all ye deeps; fire and hail, snow and vapours, stormy wind fulfilling his word, mountains and all hills; fruitful trees and all cedars; beasts and all cattle; creeping things and winged fowl! Kings of the earth and all peoples, princes and all judges of the earth; both young men and maidens, old men and children; let them praise the name of YHVH! For his name alone is exalted; his glory is above the earth and heaven . . . ' (Psalms 148).

For the prophet-king, the synonym of this universal praise is either the call to the 'great name', *Yah*, or the call to the 'complete name', YHVH;[1] this is why his exhortation begins with the words: 'Praise *Yah*! Praise YHVH! . . . ' This universal invocation is made up of the indefinite multitude of modes in which the divine voice chooses to speak through his 'organs' which are his creatures; however, where all worlds, all beings, all things emerge directly from their first and divine unity, that is, from *Yah* 'who rides on *Araboth*', there is only one mode of invocation, a single sound, a single cry, which expresses the joy of myriads of creatures in union with the One, the Unique. For where all beings issue from God is the place where all return to him without delay; here, on the 'surface of the waters', in the seventh heaven, *Araboth*, all that becomes separated from the Lord is separated only in order to be reunited with him. In effect, his creative act and his redemptive act are experienced there as one and the same thing: thanks to separation from him, union with him takes place.

Beings emerge like so many 'sparks' from the irradiation of the *shekhinah*, that is to say of *metatron*, the divine 'sun' which contains them all in so far as they are immanent and unseparated archetypes. On leaving this luminous world, where all is one with God, the sparks become enveloped in the differentiated manifestation of *avir*, that is, in the subtle 'waters' of the seventh heaven, over the surface of which the 'wind of *Elohim*' breathes and produces innumerable 'waves'. This wind is the cosmic spirit, *metatron*, which sets *avir*, the universal substance, in motion in order for it to produce subtle 'waves', that is, souls each one of which is animated, illuminated and inhabited by a spiritual 'spark', a 'living being'. Each 'wave' appearing on the 'surface of the waters', whether issuing from God or returning from the depths of the cosmic 'ocean', bursts into a single cry of joy and expands over the whole extent of the existential sea, the whole of *Araboth*.

[1] The name *Yah* is the direct and synthetic articulation of the 'primordial sound', whereas the name YHVH is the indirect and 'explicit' articulation of the same; every holy name moreover represents a more or less explicit utterance of the divine voice, but to a lesser degree than the name YHVH.

Over this hovers the eighth heaven, *avir*, the undifferentiated and translucid ether, which is wholly penetrated by the spiritual sun, *metatron*, so that the whole firmament itself appears like a sun, illuminating the 'surface of the waters' from one end to the other. As we have said, each 'wave' produced on this surface instantly expands in the supreme invocation and becomes the whole of the indefinite expanse, the immense 'mirror', which is so filled with divine light that it mingles – in essential 'fusion' and not in qualitative 'confusion' – with the 'radiant face' of *Yah* inclined towards it. Thus each being is simultaneously united with the whole of existence and with the infinite source of existence.

But if it is said that this integral union takes place at the very instant when the created being issues from uncreated being, one may wonder how the being then descends to the lower heavens and down to this earth in the form of a separate individual or separate 'world'. This descent takes place as follows: The 'fine upper point' of the created being, which is its spiritual or divine 'spark', remains in the seventh heaven in constant fusion with the infinite light of God, whilst its extension downwards – inwardly a spiritual vibration, outwardly a subtle 'wave' – begins to expand on the 'surface of the waters' and descend into the midst of the cosmic 'ocean', there to follow its predestined path. The created being is similar in this way to a letter of the Hebrew alphabet, which, starting from its upper point, opens out first in the form of a horizontal stroke and is prolonged in one fashion or another in the direction of its lower limit. Just as letters, when pronounced, return to their origin – the silent world of the uncreated and creative Word – so do animate beings or subtle 'waves', having issued with the 'primordial sound' from the divine silence and having vibrated through the heavens as far as here below, then return from their terrestrial end-point towards their celestial point of departure, from which they have never been separated and which is itself in permanent union with God.

We have seen that all created beings without exception issue through the same invocation – the 'primordial sound' – from their divine origin and return to it through this same 'cry for joy'. This simultaneously creative and redemptive sound is heard when the vibration of the divine light falls on the first subtle and cosmic expanse of the ether, on the 'surface of the waters'. Each of the waves formed therein truly 'bursts' with joy and is nothing but an exclamation of gladness which expands over the whole of *Araboth*; each being there is just a 'voice' vibrating with bliss, joined with all the other 'cries' in the one 'voice of YHVH' which 'resounds over the waters' (Psalms 29:3). This 'voice', this first and universal sound, expressed simultaneously by the Creator and by all his creatures, is symbolized in sacred ideophony by the vowel *a*; this issues from the *y (yod)*—from the unity of *shekhinah-metatron* —and spreads out indefinitely to the confines of the existential 'ocean', through the *h (he)* or *avir,* that 'very pure and impercep- tible air' coming from the mouth of God. Such is the genesis of the divine great name, *Yah,* of which it is said (Psalms 150:6): 'Let everything that hath breath praise Yah! *Halaluyah!* (praised be *Yah*).[1]

God, by invoking his creative and redemptive name, causes everything that exists to issue from him and to return into him; by invoking his name with him, every being is born from him, lives by him, and is united with him.

[1] In The Apocalypse (19:6–7) there is also an allusion to the invocation of *Yah* by the 'waters' of the cosmic ocean; St John speaks of their 'voice' which says *Hallelujah*! and of the redemptive joy which goes with the invocation: 'And I heard as it were the voice of a great multitude and as the voice of many waters, and as the voice of mighty thunderings, saying: Hallelujah: for the Lord God omnipotent reigneth!'

Let us remember that 'Hallelujah' represents not only a form of invocation of *Yah* in Judaism, but also became, by way of the Psalms, a praise of God in the Christian tradition.

IX Conclusion

Union with the divinity was shown in the union experienced by Israel on Sinai when God revealed himself. All degrees of existence, from the highest to the lowest, appeared to the Chosen People integrated and transfigured in the single 'glory' or omnipresence of God, this being moreover infinitely united with his transcendental essence: all made but one in the evidence of the causal and universal interconnection of all things and their essential identity with the Supreme. Such is the vision of the world for him who knows God, and such shall be the universal state actualized in the final redemption. The great Kabbalistic master, Moses de Leon, spoke of it in his *Sefer Harimmon*: 'Every thing is linked with another down to the very lowest link of the chain and the true essence of God is above as well as below, in the heavens and on the earth, and nothing exists outside of him. This is what the wise men mean when they say: "When God gave the Torah to the Israelites, He opened the seven heavens to them and they saw that nothing was really there but his glory (or presence); he opened the seven worlds (or earths) to them and they saw nothing there but his glory; he opened the seven abysses (or hells) before their eyes and they saw there was nothing there but his glory. Meditate on these things and you will understand that the essence of God is connected with all these worlds and that all forms of existence are connected together but derive from the existence and the essence of God."

God is the 'One without second' and could not wish anything other than himself, in himself and in all that which, being his, may take on the appearance of 'other than him'. If he wished 'something other', he would not be the One, the only reality. That is why his being and all it comprises, all that exists, desires nothing other than him; and this is true of the very least of creatures, whether they be conscious of it or not. Everything animate is looking for him, through some participation in his reality, no matter what. But the 'illusion' of the creature consists in mistaking transitory participation for the whole of reality, in confusing the finite with the infinite.

The true and divine will of the created is expressed in its thirst for the absolute, its desire for freedom from all limitation, its search for the only truth, the only reality. The infinite seeks itself through the finite.

However, though the divine 'self' desires itself in the midst of the 'me', not every human individual is receptive to 'God's search', or in equal degree. True wisdom is only to be found in one who directs both his thought and his will – his entire being – towards the real; he manifests the supreme wisdom which is simultaneously 'being', 'thought', and 'will'. This divine search leads man to identification of his qualities and his being with the perfections and being of God; it leads to his 'deification'. But in the traditional view of Judaism, the fear of God predominates – to guard against any possible confusion between the finite and the infinite – and the idea of deification is supplanted by that of 'sanctification'; thanks to sanctification, the human being is purified and penetrated by the divine in order that this may cause him to go beyond his limits and 'deliver' his essence.

'Be holy, for I am holy, I YHVH, your God' (Leviticus 19:2). All the perfections of God can be summed up in his sanctity, manifested on the human plane as the archetype of 'deiformity' and as the essence of 'deification'. The 'outer' or individual man is a 'form'; therefore he could never be more than 'deiform'. But the 'inner' man surpasses the individual-human form; our innermost and purely spiritual being is universal in nature; it can be made whole, 'deified', even to union with the essence.

Thus, sanctification implies, beyond its partial and preparatory applications, union of man with the 'Holy One' himself. The question arises: Is access to the way of sanctification possible in an 'Edomite' world like our own? The *Zohar* (*Shemoth* 7b) answers: 'Alas . . . for him who will live at that time! Yet happy he who will live at that time! . . . (and) who will be found faithful at that

time! For he shall see the joy-giving light of the (divine) King!'
The *Zohar* is referring here to the period when 'time' is nearing its
'end' and nearing, therefore, the advent of the Messiah. At this
moment in the cycle which, according to all orthodox traditions,
is the one in which we are living, divine mercy must come to
lighten the spiritual darkness with 'alleviating' grace; hence-
forward, steadfast faith in God is the equivalent, for man, to the
many acts of devotion he was bound to perform in times gone by
in order to obtain the eternal 'joy bestowed by the light of the
king'. In the same sense, the divine 'mysteries of wisdom', which
for centuries were only taught 'from the mouth to the ear'
amongst the elect of the various sacred cultures, are being divul-
ged more and more in a traditional literature growing from the
soil of all the religions of the world. 'The Holy One, blessed be
he', says the *Zohar* (*Vayera* 118a), 'does not desire that so much
should be revealed to the world; but when the days of the Messiah will be at hand, even children will discover the secrets of
wisdom . . . at that time, it will be revealed to all, as it is written
(Zephaniah, 3:9): "For then will I turn to the peoples pure language that they may invoke the name of the Lord, to serve him
in unanimous submission."'

Through submission to God's only truth and reality, mankind
will find its salvation; and it is in the invoking of his name that
those who are thirsty will be rewarded with his real and deifying
presence, as the Psalmist affirms (145:18): 'The Lord is nigh unto
all them who invoke him, to all that invoke him in truth.'

Transcription

For the purposes of this book, one of the simple systems of transliteration of the Hebrew alphabet has been chosen, which, together with the numerical values of the letters, is tabulated below.

Numerical value	Letter	Name	Transcription
1	א	alef	according to vocalization
2	ב	beth	v or b (בּ)
3	ג	gimel	g
4	ד	daleth	d
5	ה	he	h
6	ו	vav	v (u or o when used as a vowel)
7	ז	zayin	z
8	ח	heth	h
9	ט	teth	t
10	י	yod	y (by itself or before a vowel, otherwise i)
20	כ	kaf	kh or k (כּ)
30	ל	lamed	l
40	מ	mem	m
50	נ	nun	n
60	ס	samekh	s
70	ע	ayin	according to vocalization
80	פ	fe or pe	f or p (פּ)
90	צ	tsade	ts
100	ק	qof	k
200	ר	resh	r
300	ש	sin or shin	s (שׂ) or sh (שׁ)
400	ת	thaw or taw	th or t (תּ)

Index

Some other books published by Penguin
are described on the following pages.

René Guénon

THE REIGN OF QUANTITY
AND THE SIGNS OF THE TIMES

The Reign of Quantity is a condemnation of the
modern world from the point of view of an "ancient
wisdom" once common to both East and West but
now almost entirely lost. In this unique book the
late René Guénon attacks the very basis of modern
civilization with its industrial societies and its no-
tions of progress and evolution. In particular, he
shows that contemporary science and social science
are dominated by a quantitative approach while
neglecting the idea of quality. To this "reign of
quantity" Guénon opposes the science of the
ancient world, which he sees as rooted in divine
truth—the origin and end of all real tradition and
all true religion.

Frithjof Schuon

UNDERSTANDING ISLAM

In this interpretation of Islam for the Western, non-Moslem reader the author emphasizes Islam's timeless quality, presenting it, as it were, from within. Four fundamentals are considered: the nature of the Islamic perspective; the doctrine about, and the function of, the Quran; the role of the Prophet; and Sufism and the path of spiritual ascent. Throughout, frequent reference is made to Christian doctrine, and points of both similarity and difference are stressed. Of the first of Frithjof Schuon's books to appear in English, T. S. Eliot wrote that he had met no more impressive work in the field of the comparative study of oriental and occidental religion.

Maurice Nicoll

THE NEW MAN
An Interpretation of Some Parables and Miracles of Christ

"All sacred writings contain an outer and an inner meaning," writes Dr. Nicoll. "Behind the literal words lies another range of meaning, another form of knowledge." Penetrating in a unique fashion to this inner knowledge, he finds that the Gospels are about transcending the violence that characterizes mankind's present level of being. Indeed, they affirm the possibility of human development to a level beyond violence. Such must be the goal of humanity, and he who reaches this level is "the new man." The late Maurice Nicoll was an eminent British pioneer in psychological medicine, a pupil of Carl Jung, and after 1921, a brilliant exponent of the ideas of G. I. Gurdjieff and P. D. Ouspensky.